FROM CARMARTHEN TO KARABAGH:
A WELSH DISCOVERY OF ARMENIA

By the same author:

From Carmarthen to Karabagh:
a Welsh discovery of Armenia

Patrick Thomas

First published in 2012

© Patrick Thomas

© Gwasg Carreg Gwalch 2012

Published with the financial support
of the Welsh Books Council

ISBN: 978-1-84527-366-8

Cover design: Welsh Books Council

Published by Gwasg Carreg Gwalch,
12 Iard yr Orsaf, Llanrwst, Wales LL26 0EH
tel: 01492 642031
fax: 01492 641502
email: books@carreg-gwalch.com
website: www.carreg-gwalch.com

Cyflwynedig i John Torosyan ac Armeniaid Cymru
ac
Eilian Williams a Chyfeillion Cymreig Armenia

Dedicated to John Torosyan and the Armenians of Wales
and
Eilian Williams and the Welsh Friends of Armenia

To help Armenia is to help civilization.

W. E. Gladstone

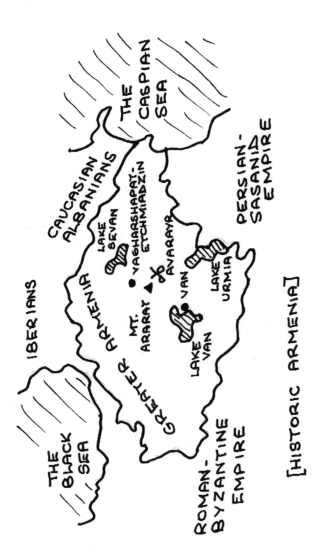

Historic Armenia

Acknowledgements

My sincere thanks to Myrddin ap Dafydd and Jen Llywelyn of Gwasg Carreg Gwalch for their unstinting support with what must have seemed at times a wildly improbable project. I would also like to express my appreciation to the Welsh Books Council for providing a publication grant, and to Mr John Shirley, who suggested that I apply to the Isla Johnson Trust, which generously funded a journey to some of the more remote areas of Armenia and Nagorno-Karabagh.

A great many people have assisted me over the past few years, many in ways of which they are probably completely unaware. Although I do not have the space to name them all, I am particularly grateful to Naira Alaverdyan, Baroness Caroline Cox, Canon Hugh Wybrew, Archbishop Rowan Williams and Bishop Vahan Hovhanessian (who graciously provided the forewords) and John Torosyan and Eilian Williams (to whom this book is dedicated). I would also like to thank the Armenian Apostolic Orthodox congregations in Cardiff and London for making me so welcome whenever I have visited and gone on pilgrimage with them, my own long-suffering flock in Christ Church/Eglwys Crist, Carmarthen, and Bishop Wyn Evans for his support and friendship and remarkable patience and forbearance with his Armenia-loving priest.

Writing about Armenia has its difficulties for a writer based in west Wales. For the last few years my wife, Helen, kindly allowed me to spend all my disposable income on books about the subject. These came from booksellers across the globe, and were brought to the vicarage by a valiant postman regularly staggering under the weight of hefty tomes from unlikely places.

Both Helen and our five children (Iori, Gareth, Llinos, Mair and Gwenllian), my four sisters (Mandy, Buffy, Vicky and Lottie), and my mother (Mrs Dilys Thomas) have been a constant source of encouragement. I am also indebted to the various groups and organisations that have invited me to give lectures and talks on Armenia in recent years, and especially to the Cistercian monks of Caldey Island.

The translations from Welsh and French are my own.

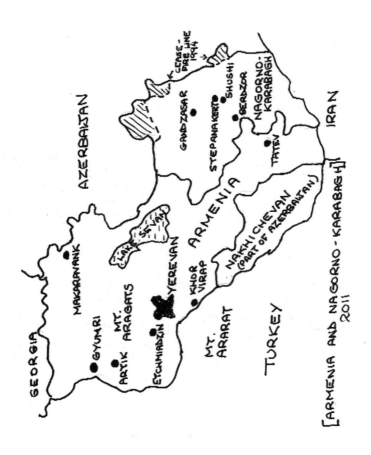

Armenia and Armenia-Nagorno-Karabagh 2011

Contents

Foreword

Dr Rowan Williams
Archbishop of Canterbury

Patrick Thomas' distinctive voice – learned, thoughtful, compassionate and witty – has become more and more widely known and appreciated through his writings about Wales and the imaginative legacy of Christian faith in Wales. Here he turns to another subject, though without at all leaving behind his characteristic rootedness in the local realities of Carmarthenshire. His love affair with Armenia began, as he tells us, some six years ago, and it has worked itself out through many visits, through passionate advocacy and through a deep immersion in the culture of this extraordinary nation. Unsurprisingly, he finds analogies with another small and mountainous country, jealous of its language and its heritage. And in these pages he introduces us to some of the most poignant and beautiful literature of the Armenians, shaped as it is by a history of appalling suffering.

The great national trauma that overtook the Armenian people at the beginning of the twentieth century produced its own depth of protest, its own echoes of the Psalmist's loud cries of anger and pain towards God. Patrick Thomas introduce us not only to the history of this tragedy but to some of the individuals, the poets, who struggled to find the words that would communicate to the world what had been endured. Many readers will, I suspect, find these pages the most haunting in the book. But they would make no sense without the history that goes before, and the author gives us a warm and vivid portrait in a brief space of the richness of Armenian Christianity.

Ultimately, the message – the plea – is that we should recognise the near-sacramental significance of the small nation and the 'minority' language. Every people and language offers a distinctive perspective on the common task of being human; how much more in the family of Christ's Body! To say this does not commit anyone to anxious and exclusive nationalism, let alone to the poisonous myths of race. But just as each person shows a particular facet of the shared truth of Christ, so does each local community and each bit of history received and remembered in those communities. In this moving little book, we see how that shared truth was received in the long history of faith in Armenia, and something of the good news that its people have to give us even today – a word of hope and even joy out of what the Bible calls the 'iron furnace' of collective suffering.

+ Rowan Cantuar:
Lambeth Palace
Ascensiontide, 2011

Foreword

His Grace Bishop Vahan Hovhanessian, Primate of the Armenian Apostolic Orthodox Church in Britain and Ireland

Unlike the early and medieval literature in the West, today rarely do we come across writings in English that explore the culture and history of the Armenian people, whose kingdom in AD 301 was the first in the world to adopt Christianity as the state religion. In fact, in certain cases, one cannot but wonder about the reason for the inexplicable and painful silence of the contemporary media, journalists and historians vis-à-vis the atrocities and injustices committed against the Armenians. Canon Patrick Thomas, however, is known to be a voice of the voiceless and a true disciple of the Lord whose life is a demonstration of the apostolic command, 'Beloved, whatever is true, whatever is honourable, whatever is just, whatever is pure, whatever is pleasing, whatever is commendable, if there is any excellence and if there is anything worthy of praise, think about these things' (Philippians 4:8). Canon Patrick's book is truly one of these literary jewels that not only sheds light on the history, culture and literature of the Armenians but sets it up against the beautifully complementing and surprisingly parallel background of the Welsh people's history and experience. By doing so, Canon Patrick offers the reader a harmonious tale of two thousand years of Christian testimony and witnessing of these two nations.

Following the introduction to the book, Canon Patrick takes us through an inspiring journey from Camarthen to Karabagh. The story is a narration of actual journeys the author has undertaken to explore Armenia and the Armenian people. Canon Patrick beautifully interlaces key events and traditions in the history of the Armenian people, offering an introduction to the Armenians and their homeland, which in itself makes his book a valuable resource to Armenian and non-Armenian readers alike. Furthermore, the Welsh context in which he presents the Armenian experiences, and the Welsh perspectives in analysing these events, makes this volume truly a unique and valuable publication.

In his humility, and referring to himself at the conclusion of the introduction to the book, Canon Patrick Thomas states, 'Writing about a culture from outside is always a difficult and sensitive process.' However, those of us who know Canon Patrick well also know that in his spirit, through his many travels to Armenia and Karabagh, his passion to learn more about the culture and history of the Armenians and pursue the parallel between the Armenian and Welsh people, and his continuous support of the rights of the Armenians in contemporary issues, Canon Patrick has earned the right to be an honorary ambassador of the Armenian people to the rest of the world.

On behalf of the Armenians in the United Kingdom and the Republic of Ireland we thank Canon Patrick Thomas for his research and publications in support of the Armenian people, and congratulate him on the occasion of the publication of this indispensable volume. May the Lord continue blessing him, his family and his ministry.

In Christ's service,

Bishop Vahan Hovhanessian
Diocese of the Armenian Church of Britain and Ireland
30 November 2011

Introduction

Why Armenia?

In the early summer of 2005 I was leafing through the back pages of the *Church Times*, when a small advertisement caught my eye. 'Father Hugh is leading a pilgrimage to Armenia,' I remarked to my wife. Canon Hugh Wybrew had been Helen's parish priest in Pinner, Middlesex, and was the sort of Anglo-Catholic cleric whom I have always found rather unnerving: suave, sophisticated, scholarly, precise in all things, adept at ceremonial, with not a hair out of place. Both my mother-in-law and my wife regarded him as their ideal of what a priest should be like.

Helen glanced at the *Church Times* advertisement. 'You'd better go,' she said. 'It'll do you good and Father Hugh will make sure that you won't get lost.' She was right on both counts. My first visit to Armenia, in October 2005, was a revelation. I was introduced to a country that had an extraordinarily rich culture, influenced by both Europe and Asia. Its people had faced the most appalling horrors over the centuries: invasions, massacres, religious persecution, political oppression, deportations, earthquakes and genocide. Nevertheless, they had managed to preserve their identity, their language and alphabet, and their unique strand of Christianity, with its powerful symbolism and mystical poetry. Father Hugh turned out to be charming, witty and informative, and by the end of the pilgrimage I was no longer quite so much in awe of him.

On my return I immersed myself in books about Armenian history, religion and culture. My second son, worried that his father was turning into a chronic Armeno-bore, suggested that I should be fined 50p whenever I mentioned Armenia at meal-times. My mother was astonished by the pilgrimage's impact on me, and kindly helped to finance another visit. In September 2006 I landed once again at Zvartnots International Airport outside Yerevan, the Armenian capital. This time I was not in a group. Naira Alaverdyan, my lively and highly intelligent tour guide and interpreter, proved to be a wonderful source of information about every aspect of Armenian life. I visited the south of the country for the first time, seeing the majestic monastery of Tatev and the prehistoric observatory at Karahunj (the 'Armenian Stonehenge').

By now I was becoming increasingly aware of the intriguing parallels and contrasts between Armenia and Wales. As a result of an article I wrote for *Cambria* magazine, Eilian Williams, the indefatigable and courageous human rights campaigner, invited me to speak during the unveiling of the Armenian Genocide Memorial at the Temple of Peace in Cardiff in November 2007. The Turkish and British governments (unlike the Welsh Assembly) still refuse to recognise the genocide, and the event was picketed by a noisy crowd of extreme Turkish nationalists. The Armenians greeted my speech with enthusiasm and made sure that the text appeared on the internet.

John Shirley, the Provincial Secretary of the Church in Wales, informed me that I was eligible for a grant from the Isla Johnson Trust to further my study of Armenia. The trustees responded with great generosity. In May 2008 I was back in the country, intending to reach some remoter areas and cross over into the Republic of Nagorno-Karabagh, the Armenian enclave that broke away from Azerbaijan during a bitter struggle in the 1990s. My experiences inspired a sequence of 'Prayer for the Day' meditations that were broadcast on BBC Radio 4.

A fourth opportunity to visit Armenia arose in September 2009. I joined another pilgrimage, this time led by Baroness Caroline Cox. Caroline is an impressive but slightly terrifying combination of Florence Nightingale, Margaret Thatcher and Joan of Arc: forthright, determined and with nerves of steel. During the Nagorno-Karabagh war, at a time when the embattled Armenians felt ignored or forgotten by everyone except their fellow Armenians abroad, she championed their cause and shared their hardships, risking her life on many occasions to bring them medical supplies. The result is that in Armenia, and particularly in Nagorno-Karabagh, Caroline is regarded as a national hero. 'She is our sister!' people kept exclaiming. Someone even told me that the Armenian Patriarch of Jerusalem hopes eventually to secure her bones as sacred relics.

Being on a pilgrimage with Caroline meant that we met people whom we might otherwise not have met, and went to places where we might otherwise not have gone. In Stepanakert we had dinner with the Archbishop of Artsakh, the leader of the Armenian Church in Nagorno-Karabagh. In Holy Etchmiadzin, the spiritual centre of the Armenian Church, we sat in places of honour next to His Holiness Karekin II, the Catholicos of All Armenians, during a celebration of the *Badarak* (the Armenian Liturgy), and afterwards had an audience with him in his residence. We also visited a seminary at Lake Sevan where young men were training for the Armenian priesthood.

In 2010 the Armenian community in Cardiff invited me to their Genocide Commemoration. It was an opportunity to meet the Very Reverend Dr Vahan Hovhanessian, the new Primate of the Armenian Church in Britain and Ireland. As a welcoming gift I presented him with a slate copy of the Celtic Cross on the Abraham Stone at St David's, which bears a striking resemblance to a cross in a medieval illuminated manuscript from Artsakh (Nagorno-Karabagh). In return he presented me with a beautifully carved marble *khatchkar* (cross-stone) from Holy Etchmiadzin, which I now keep beside my prayer desk in Christ Church, Carmarthen.

Later that year Father Vahan visited St David's Cathedral at my invitation. The following day I attended what was probably the first-ever celebration of the *Badarak* in Wales, which, appropriately enough, was held at Ararat Baptist Church in Cardiff (Mount Ararat was historically in Armenia). It was a moving and joyful occasion. We began to make plans for an Armenian pilgrimage to St David's, as the Mother Church of the People of Wales. This took place shortly after Easter 2011, and included both a celebration of the *Badarak* and a commemoration of the Armenian Genocide.

Armenian Christmas ('Theophany') is on 6 January and celebrates both the birth and the baptism of Christ, following the early Christian tradition. The first Armenian Christmas services in Wales were held in Ararat Baptist Church on 8 January 2011. Father Vahan brought a choir from London, and Father Karekin (a young Armenian priest who is doing research at Sheffield University), celebrated the *Badarak*, assisted by Senior Deacon Levon (a genial vet from Exeter). The Armenian chanting was ethereal, and the atmosphere it created was a wonderfully numinous expression of the beauty of holiness. I later discovered that Father Karekin had been the celebrant at the *Badarak* in Holy Etchmiadzin where I had been placed next to the Catholicos. *Mae'r byd yn fach!*

After the *Badarak* Father Vahan performed the Blessing of Water, which commemorates the Baptism of Christ. John Torosyan, the genial and delightful father figure of the Welsh Armenian community, was given the role of godfather, holding a silver cross during the ceremony. The water is mixed with *muron*, the sweet-scented oil of chrism made from Armenian flowers. New *muron* is blessed by the Catholicos in a special ceremony at Etchmiadzin once every seven years. Some of the old *muron* is mixed with the fresh chrism, ensuring a continuity that goes all the way back to St Gregory the Enlightener, who converted Armenia to Christianity in 301. Drinking this sacred mixture in Cardiff we became indissolubly linked to over 1700 years of Armenian Christian tradition and witness.

* * *

Wales and Armenia are two small mountainous countries at either end of what was once regarded as Christendom. The head waiter at a restaurant on the shores of Lake Sevan in Armenia remarked enthusiastically when he heard where I came from that 'Wales is an ancient country, like Armenia.' He added: 'We have both had to struggle a long time for our freedom.' Visiting, learning and writing about Armenia has given me a deeper understanding of the culture and spiritual heritage of my own country. As the Russian writer Kim Bakshi has put it:

... every people must have at least one friend who comes from another people, a person who loves and knows them, who can work for them for a long time, seeks no recognition, and will come to their aid when necessary.

When you can be a friend to another people, can give up your stereotypes and biases, you are defending the honour of your own people.

When I look at the Armenian people with love and understanding I realize that this is a wonderful mirror in which I can see my own people all the better, our history, spiritual wealth, and the Christian path that we once travelled together.[1]

This book begins with a short introduction to the history of Armenia. The chapters that follow have a structure that stems from aspects of Armenian and Welsh cultural tradition. The theme of each one is established by a prologue. This is the equivalent of the illuminated canon tables in medieval Armenian Gospel-books, which form a kind of arcade through which the reader passes into the Gospels themselves. An Armenian 'triad' follows, based on the pattern of the *Trioedd Ynys Prydein* used by medieval Welsh story-tellers. Finally there is a 'colophon'. Armenian colophons are additions made to manuscripts by their scribes or owners, often commenting on the history of the time or the conditions in which the work was copied or preserved. In this book the colophons are reflections from a Welsh standpoint on what has gone before. It's a unique, slightly eccentric, but very deliberate framework, which is intended to combine both characteristically Armenian and Welsh elements.

A note on transliteration

Armenian has its own alphabet and transliteration is notoriously problematic (particularly because of differences between Western and Eastern Armenian). An extreme example is given by Anne Avakian. Referring to Servantsian, the father of Armenian folklore, she notes that she has come across thirty-nine different spellings of his name in her research.[2] For this book I have chosen the forms of names that are most familiar to me, and have attempted to be consistent. I have not included diacritical marks, except where these occur in the titles of books referred to in footnotes. I apologise sincerely if I have unwittingly made any mistakes or trodden on any toes in the process.

Writing about a culture from outside is always a difficult and sensitive process. I am very conscious that as an *odar* (a non-Armenian) I may have inadvertently committed all sorts of blunders and been guilty of misunderstandings or misapprehension. I hope that any Armenian readers will forgive such errors and appreciate that they are certainly not intentional – but I look forward to having any mistakes courteously but firmly corrected by my kind Armenian friends.

Patrick Thomas
Carmarthen, Wales
January 2012

Notes

1 Kim Bakshi, *The Resurrection of Saint Lazarus* (Venice: Mekhitarian Centre of Armenia, 1998), p. 16.
2 Anne M. Avakian, *Armenian Folklore Bibliography* (Berkeley: University of California Press, 1994), p. xii.

Prologue
A short history of Armenia

i) Place and people

The land-locked and mountainous Armenian Republic has present-day borders with Turkey, Georgia, Azerbaijan and Iran. Its territory is roughly a third greater than that of Wales, while the populations of the two countries are broadly similar. However, as Armenians are quick to emphasize, the present country is only about a tenth of the size of Historic Armenia. Its borders once extended into a large area of what is now Eastern Turkey. During the medieval period there was also an Armenian kingdom in Cilicia on the shores of the Mediterranean.

Today a diaspora of some four million Armenians live outside the country's borders. Many of them are descendants of survivors from the genocide that wiped out over a million Turkish Armenians during the First World War. There are major Armenian communities in the United States (especially California), Russia, France, Lebanon and Iran. In Britain there are well-established Armenian Churches in London and Manchester, which act as a focus for religious and cultural activities. The Armenian community in Cardiff has played a central part in ensuring the Welsh Assembly's recognition of the Armenian Genocide and the erection of a memorial to its victims in the garden of the Temple of Peace.

On my first visit to Armenia I sat in a restaurant in Yerevan listening to a folk musician playing the duduk, a hauntingly mournful flute that is one of the country's most distinctive instruments. The eyes of Aram, our

Armenian guide, suddenly filled with tears. 'Our history is so sad,' he said. 'First there is one invasion, and then another invasion, and then another invasion ...' Armenia's geographical position has made it the focus of an almost constant clash of civilisations.

Robert Hewsen's atlas of Armenian history contains a map that graphically illustrates this. It shows Hittites, Macedonians, Romans, Byzantines, Crusaders and Ottoman Turks coming from the west; Assyrians, Arabs and Egyptian Mamlukes from the south-west; Medes, Persians, Parthians, Seljuk Turks and Mongols from the south east, and from the north Cimmerians, Scythians, Alans, Khazars, Georgians, Russians and Soviets. In wave after wave they each in their turn converged on Armenia over the centuries.[1]

The human cost of these invasions was often appalling. But the geographical accident that made Armenia the victim of rival empires and savage conquerors was not wholly negative. It meant that the country and its people developed a unique and rich culture. Armenia became the meeting point of East and West, of Europe and Asia. It drew on the different streams that flowed through it, transforming and transmuting them into something that was, and is, very much its own.

Three factors played a significant part in this. The first is the Armenian language. Armenian, like Welsh, is an Indo-European language. We still share a handful of words that must go back into the very distant past. The beautiful Armenian alphabet created by St Mesrop Mashtots at the beginning of the fifth century was also important. Its thirty-eight letters are not easy to master – the task almost broke Lord Byron's heart when he first had a stab at it. 'You know the letters!' an

Armenian companion exclaimed in amazement when I began to spell out the name of a building in Yerevan. I have to confess that I still occasionally get caught out by some of them.

The third major element that has helped to preserve and strengthen Armenian identity is religious faith. Tradition claims that Christianity was first brought to Armenia by Saints Bartholomew and Thaddeus, two of Christ's apostles. It only had a minority following until 301 or thereabouts, when, through the heroic mission of St Gregory the Illuminator, Armenia became the first country to recognise Christianity as its state religion. Persecution followed. Zoroastrians, Muslims and Soviet atheists have all failed to undermine Armenia's Christian identity. Greek and Russian Orthodox and the Roman Catholics have also been unsuccessful in their attempts to take over the Armenian Apostolic Church. It retains a liturgy, theology and culture that make it a unique and special expression of the Christian faith.

ii) Origins

Most nations have a legendary version of their origins. As late as 1740 the scholarly Theophilus Evans still traced Welsh beginnings back to Gomer, Noah's grandson. He was said to have spoken 'Gomeraeg', which later became 'Cymraeg' (Welsh). Armenians call their country 'Haiastan' after its mythological founder, Haik. He was Gomer's great-grandson, which means that (in the realms of legend at any rate) the Welsh and the Armenians share a common ancestor.

The early Armenian historian Moses Khorenatsi describes Haik as 'handsome and personable, with curly hair, sparkling eyes and strong arms'.[2] This attractive hero lived in Babylon, under the oppressive rule of a tyrant named Bel. Fed up with being bullied, Haik returned to the region where his ancestor Noah had landed from the Ark. Bel pursued the fugitive. The two gigantic men fought each other and the tyrant was killed. Haik and his descendants then settled in Haiastan.

The complexities of history are more obscure and often rather less satisfying than mythological accounts. The earliest reference to Armenia is in the sixth century BC. Three hundred years later it threw off its Median overlords and became an independent state. By 80 BC it was (briefly) a significant political force. Tigran the Great exploited the internal difficulties of the two superpowers: Rome and Parthian-ruled Persia. Stepping into the vacuum, he created an Armenian Empire which stretched from the Caspian Sea to the Mediterranean. The Romans sorted themselves out and hit back. By 66 BC they had shorn Tigran of most of his conquests. Armenia was left as a buffer state between the Parthians and the Romans, allied to the latter.

A further complication emerged around the year 301, when St Gregory the Illuminator converted the Armenian King Trdat III and his country became the first officially Christian state. The Sasanids, rulers of Persia since 224, were enthusiastic Zoroastrians who regarded this development with some unease. While the Roman emperors remained aggressively pagan it was less of a problem, but when Constantine the Great adopted the Christian faith the Armenians became progressively more suspect in the eyes of the Sasanids.

At the beginning of the fifth century St Mesrop Mashtots invented an alphabet for the Armenian language. This triggered an explosion of literary activity, with the translation of Greek and Syriac texts (beginning with the Bible), as well as the production of original material. The century became known as the 'Golden Age' of Armenian literature. It was a development which came at a crucial time. Armenia had been divided between the Byzantines and the Sasanid Persians, and by 428 both parts had been absorbed into the empires of their respective overlords. It was not long before the Sasanid ruler decided to impose Zoroastrianism on his Armenian Christian subjects.

The Armenian resistance was led by a hereditary general named Vardan Mamikonian. In 451 he inflicted huge losses on a massive Persian army at the battle of Avarayr. Vardan and many of his companions were killed during the fighting. From the day of their death they have been venerated as saints and martyrs by the Armenian Church. Years of bitter guerrilla warfare followed. Eventually in 484 the Persians relented and allowed the Armenians freedom to worship in their own way. Friction with their fellow Christians would soon follow.

While the Armenians were battling for survival against the Persians, the other Christian churches met at the Council of Chalcedon to attempt to define the relationship between Christ's humanity and divinity. By 555 the Armenian Church had firmly rejected the decrees of Chalcedon, setting themselves apart from both Rome and Byzantium. The religious and political consequences of this decision helped to shape both the future of Armenian history and the nature of Armenian individuality and identity.

iii) The Middle Ages
In the opening decades of the seventh century the

Byzantines and the Sasanid Persians were too busy fighting each other to notice the dramatic emergence of a third force on the Arabian peninsula. Suddenly the hosts of Islam swept northwards, overwhelming the two exhausted empires. The Sasanids were destroyed and the Byzantines were pushed back towards the west. In 652 the leading Armenian nobleman made peace with the Arab invaders. The result was a half-century of stability during which some of the finest examples of Armenian religious architecture were produced.

However, Arab rule became increasingly oppressive, sparking several Armenian rebellions. Many leading noble families were weakened or wiped out in these conflicts. A few were still powerful enough to take advantage of divisions among the Arabs towards the end of the ninth century. The Bagratuni family founded an Armenian kingdom, whose eventual capital was Ani. This 'city of a thousand churches', whose ruins are now on the Turkish side of the Armenian border, became famous for the beauty of its architecture, its massive defensive walls, and its dwellings both above and below ground.

A rival family, the Artsrunis, established a kingdom in Vaspurakan, the area around Lake Van. Two masterpieces emerged from this southern Armenian realm. One was the unique and fascinating Church of the Holy Cross on the island of Aghtamar. The other was the collection of prayer poems by the mystic St Grigor Narekatsi, which had a lasting influence on Armenian literature and spirituality. It was also during this period that the characteristically Armenian carving of *khatchkars* (cross-stones) began to develop into an increasingly sophisticated art form with a profound religious significance.

The rulers of Byzantium decided against using these Armenian kingdoms as buffer states to protect their empire against invaders from the east. By the early eleventh century they adopted a policy of persuading or coercing Armenian rulers into handing over their territories in exchange for lands far away from the border. Many of the people accompanied their overlords. The result was a disaster for Byzantium. The Seljuk Turks captured Ani in 1045. In 1071 they crushed the Byzantine Emperor at Manzikert. Historic Armenia was now almost entirely in Turkish hands.

Many Armenians had emigrated south towards Cilicia on the Mediterranean coast, beyond the protective barrier of the Taurus Mountains. They began to develop a degree of independence. In the closing years of the eleventh century these Cilician Armenians acquired some unexpected allies when the Crusaders marched through their territory on their way to the Holy Land. The Armenian nobility built up a close (if occasionally tempestuous) relationship with the leaders of the Crusader states, cemented by frequent intermarriage. By the end of the twelfth century Cilician Armenia was recognised as a kingdom, ruled by Levon I.

Meanwhile, the remaining nobility of Greater Armenia had allied with the Georgians to expel the Seljuk Turks. For a short but significant period two brilliant Armenian generals (the Zakarian brothers) ruled northern Armenia as vassals of the Georgians. This brief renaissance was snuffed out by a new enemy. The Mongols swept into Greater Armenia and incorporated it into their empire.

Cilician Armenia faced a different danger.

Threatened by the Egyptian Mamluks, King Hetum I decided on a startlingly imaginative diplomatic strategy. He formed an alliance with the Mongols, even travelling to their distant capital of Karakorum to confirm the agreement. The partnership worked well until the Mongol rulers, formerly not unsympathetic towards Christianity, decided to convert to Islam. As the Crusader states were successively overrun, Cilician Armenia became increasingly isolated.

The Cilician kingdom was an anomaly: an Armenian state outside Historic Armenia. Despite its political fragility it produced a cultural renaissance reflected by the 'Silver Age' poetry of Catholicos St Nerses Shnorhali, and beautiful illuminated manuscripts painted with breathtaking skill by Toros Roslin, Sargis Pidzak and other masters. In 1375 the final Cilician stronghold fell to the Mamluks. The last Armenian king died in exile in France in 1393.

Between 1386 and 1403 Timur the Lame (Tamerlane) and his armies repeatedly raided Greater Armenia in an orgy of killing and destruction. Their brutality traumatized the Armenians for generations, and is still the subject of many folk traditions and stories. The period that followed was bleak for those Armenians who remained in their homeland, faced with power struggles between their curiously named 'Black Sheep' and 'White Sheep' Turkmen overlords.

iv) Between Great Powers

Armenia has repeatedly found itself caught between rival powers. By the beginning of the sixteenth century the Ottoman Turkish Empire and the Safavid Persians confronted each other on Armenian territory. Many Armenians chose to emigrate. Others had no choice.

The most devastating deportation came in 1604–5. Shah Abbas forcibly removed a quarter of a million Armenians to Persia. Many died on the way. The deportees included some Armenian silk merchants from Julfa in Nakhichevan, whose wealth and business acumen had attracted the Shah's attention. He settled them in New Julfa, a suburb of Isfahan. They quickly developed a successful trading network that linked India and the Far East to Europe, using some of the proceeds to build several magnificent churches in their new home.

At a time when Armenian morale was at a low ebb, the seeds of a cultural renaissance were sown by a gifted hand in an unexpected place. Mkhitar Sebastatsi (1676–1749) was a celibate priest who felt called to form a scholarly religious order. Turned down by the Armenian Patriarchal authorities in Constantinople, he took his followers into the Roman Catholic Church. His Mekhitarist Order was granted the island of San Lazzaro in Venice. From there it produced Armenian grammars and dictionaries and a wide range of scholarly and popular works.

The eighteenth century also saw Russia expanding towards the Caucasus. Armenians, wearied by centuries of futile attempts to get help from the West, became aware of a possible new Christian ally. They were initially disappointed. In the 1720s the heroic fighter Davit Bek led a dogged struggle for freedom in the Armenian provinces of Zangezur and Karabagh. The anticipated support from Peter the Great of Russia never arrived. By the early nineteenth century, however, enthusiastic Armenian volunteers helped the Russians to take Eastern Armenia from Persia. Armenia still remained a battleground. The rival empires were now Russia and Ottoman Turkey.

An important cultural shift was beginning to take place. Armenian literature had formerly been written in the ancient classical language which is still used today in church services. Now a new vernacular writing, which took two forms, began to develop in cities with large Armenian populations outside the Armenian heartland. Western Armenian emerged in Constantinople among writers who often had links with France or Italy. The centre of Eastern Armenian culture was Tiflis (now Tbilisi) in Georgia. Many of its exponents had been students in Russia or Germany.

The clash of empires put those Armenians who lived in Turkey in an increasingly vulnerable position. The Russo-Turkish War of 1877–8 ended with Russian forces within striking distance of Constantinople. They had occupied almost all the Armenian provinces in Turkey. In the peace treaty that followed the Russians annexed a small part of Turkish Armenia. They were also given the right to keep troops in the remaining area until the safety of the Armenians was assured.

The British government, led by Disraeli, was furious. It saw Russian expansion as a political and commercial threat. An international congress was convened in Berlin to revise the treaty. The British persuaded the Russians to withdraw from Western Armenia and in return were given the island of Cyprus by the Turks. Mkrtich Khrimian, a fiery patriot who was the outstanding Armenian cleric of the nineteenth century, had gone to Berlin to plead his people's cause. He returned deeply disillusioned by the underhand machinations of European politicians and painfully aware of Armenian powerlessness.

Their betrayal at the Congress of Berlin left Sultan

Abdul Hamid II of Turkey free to act towards his Armenian subjects in whatever way took his fancy. Between 1895 and 1896 he instigated the systematic slaughter of Armenians in the villages and towns of Anatolia. The number massacred is estimated at between 100,000 and 200,000. Gladstone, Disraeli's old opponent, was horrified. The eighty-six year old former Prime Minister gave his last great speech in September 1896 eloquently condemning the savagery of the 'Red Sultan'. When Gladstone died two years later, grateful Armenian merchants from Manchester paid for his tomb and a stained-glass memorial window in St Deiniol's Church, Hawarden.

There was growing opposition to the brutal Sultan from among his own people. In 1908 the 'Young Turk' Committee of Union and Progress organised a coup. It was backed by many Turkish Armenians, including members from some of the Armenian political parties that had sprung up since the 1880s. Abdul Hamid was overthrown. He made an abortive attempt to regain power in 1909. During the chaos that ensued, Turkish reactionaries, apparently with the support of some Young Turks, massacred 25,000 Armenians in Cilicia. In 1913 a triumvirate of ultra-nationalist leaders took control of Ottoman Turkey. Their pan-Turkic ideology left no place for the Armenians.

Across the border, the Eastern Armenians had their own problems. The Tsarist authorities tried to impose Russification. An attempt in 1885 to close all schools teaching through the Armenian language sparked off such a furious response that the government had to back down. Then in 1903 Tsar Nicholas II ordered the confiscation by the state of all property belonging to the Armenian Church. Mkrtich Khrimian, the erstwhile

Armenian representative at the Congress of Berlin, was now the Catholicos (Supreme Patriarch) of All Armenians. His people had given him the affectionate nickname '*Hairik*' ('Little Father'). After his refusal to accept the new law they supported him with widespread strikes and demonstrations. The Tsar caved in and appointed a pro-Armenian viceroy for the Caucasus.

v) Genocide and After

The outbreak of the First World War in 1914 saw Russia and Turkey on opposing sides. Both armies contained Armenian soldiers. After the Turks invaded the Caucasus in a disastrous winter campaign, the blame for their failure was pinned on the Armenians. In 1915, with the Russian army advancing in the east and an Allied force poised to attack the Dardanelles, the Ottoman government decided to take concerted action against its Armenian subjects.

On 24 April several hundred prominent figures from Constantinople's Armenian community were arrested without warning. They included politicians, journalists, poets, novelists, teachers and churchmen. These key individuals were deported into the Turkish hinterland where all but a handful of them were killed. This carefully calculated move effectively 'beheaded' the Turkish Armenians, depriving them of their natural leaders and spokesmen.

The systematic extermination of up to a million and a half Armenians followed. Armenian conscripts in the Turkish army were disarmed and formed into labour battalions. They were often made to dig their own graves before being slaughtered. Townspeople and villagers were forced to evacuate their homes and move off in columns towards remote and arid areas of the Syrian desert. The surviving men were separated from the other deportees and murdered. The remaining women and children were raped, robbed or abducted as they staggered onwards. Many of those who were not deliberately eliminated died of hunger, exhaustion or disease. It was one of the most shameful episodes in human history and the first large-scale genocide of the twentieth century.

After the Bolshevik Revolution in 1917 Russian troops withdrew from those areas of Turkey that they had formerly occupied. By May 1918 the Turkish army was threatening Yerevan and it seemed that the only remaining fragment of Armenian territory would be obliterated. In a defiant last stand the Armenians defeated the Turks at the battle of Sardarabad. Shortly afterwards an Armenian Republic was declared, with Yerevan as its capital.

The new state was faced with massive economic and political problems, as well as having to cope with a huge influx of starving refugees from Turkish Armenia, many of whom were orphaned children. By 1920 the tiny republic found itself trapped between a Turkish nationalist force and the Soviet Red Army. After the horrors of the genocide, the Bolsheviks seemed to offer the best hope of survival. The Armenian Republic was absorbed into the Soviet state. When the border between Turkey and Soviet Armenia was fixed, two important symbols, Mount Ararat and the ruins of the medieval Armenian capital of Ani, were left on the Turkish side.

Soviet Armenia suffered during Stalin's purges. Large numbers of people died in prison or disappeared into the gulags. Victims included several of the most gifted Armenian writers and the Catholicos of the

Armenian Church. The German invasion of the Soviet Union in 1941 led to a dramatic shift in the official attitude towards the Armenian Church and people. Almost half a million Armenians joined the Red Army and around 170,000 of them lost their lives.

It has been suggested that the world's indifference towards the horrors inflicted on the Armenians during the First World War helped to shape Hitler's own genocidal policies. On the eve of war in 1939 he remarked: 'I have placed my death-head formations in readiness ... with orders for them to send to death, mercilessly and without compassion, men, women and children of Polish derivation and language. Only thus shall we gain the living space we need. Who, after all, speaks today of the annihilation of the Armenians?'[3]

During the Soviet period Nagorno-Karabagh, an area with an overwhelmingly Armenian population, was separated from Armenia and incorporated into Azerbaijan.[4] The people of the region, frustrated by decades of repression and neglect, sensed new hope with the advent of Gorbachev's policy of *perestroika*. At the beginning of 1988 they petitioned to be allowed to rejoin Armenia. The Soviet leader's refusal of this request, combined with a pogrom of Armenians in Sumgait, an industrial town in Azerbaijan, fuelled mass protests in the Armenian capital.

In December 1988 a massive earthquake in northern Armenia killed around 25,000 people and left hundreds of thousands homeless. Gorbachev's inept response led to an upsurge of Armenian nationalist feeling. Tensions were exacerbated when Armenians were massacred in Baku, the capital of Azerbaijan. Armenians fled from Azerbaijan, Azeris fled from Armenia, and a guerrilla war broke out in Nagorno-

Karabagh. The Armenian Communist Party imploded and in September 1991 Armenians voted overwhelmingly to become an independent state.

The new Republic of Armenia faced enormous difficulties. The bitter war in Nagorno-Karabagh ended with a cease-fire in 1994, though the future of the enclave has yet to be resolved. Azerbaijan and Turkey imposed an economic blockade. There were acute power shortages during a series of bitterly cold winters. The collapse of the former integrated Soviet economy led to the closure of many factories. One result was large-scale emigration.

Armenia's leaders have had to do a delicate balancing act. Russia has widespread economic interests in their country and still helps to guard the border with Turkey. Iran supplies fuel and other essential goods. The American-Armenian Diaspora is responsible for financing many crucially important infrastructure projects. Maintaining a friendly relationship with such disparate partners is extremely difficult. Yet twenty-first century Armenians can still echo in their own way the words of one of Dafydd Iwan's most famous songs: '*Er gwaetha' pawb a phopeth ry'n ni yma o hyd!*' ('In spite of everyone and everything we are still here!').

Notes

[1] Robert H. Hewsen, *Armenia: A Historical Atlas* (Chicago: University of Chicago Press, 2001), p. 15.

[2] Moses Khorenats'i, *History of the Armenians*, translated by Robert W. Thomson (Cambridge, Massachusetts: Harvard University Press, 1978), p.85.

[3] K. B. Bardakjian, *Hitler and the Armenian Genocide* (Cambridge, Massachusetts: The Zoryan Institute, 1985), p.6.

1

Ararat

The Armenian mountain

Waking up on my first morning in Armenia, I opened the curtains of my hotel room window and looked out over the city of Yerevan. In front of me was a dilapidated building from Tsarist times with a crumpled corrugated iron roof (a '*to shinc*', as we would say in west Wales). Behind it was a depressing block of Soviet era flats of a type once commonplace from East Berlin to Vladivostok. And beyond that gloomy concrete monstrosity was, amazingly, Mount Ararat (also known as 'Masis' to Armenians).

The twin snow-covered peaks of Ararat floated above several narrow layers of cloud. They seemed to represent a different level of existence, detached from the everyday reality of the dusty Armenian capital. It was easy to understand why the story of Noah had become linked to this mountain: if humanity had to have a second chance, then why shouldn't the survivors have descended from such apparently unearthly heights to the fertile earthy plain below? It was also clear why so many generations of Armenians had felt that it was blasphemous (and probably impossible) to climb Mount Ararat.

The shape of the holy mountain is mirrored by the traditional domes of Armenian churches and the characteristic black hoods that are worn by Armenian celibate priests. In the Vernissage, the open-air market in Yerevan, countless paintings of Mount Ararat are on sale. Yet, strangely enough, the mountain is often invisible, hidden behind a haze. Some visitors spend a week in Yerevan without even catching a glimpse of it. Perhaps that adds to Ararat's mystical quality: even when you cannot see it, you are aware that it is there.

The mountain haunts the dreams of Armenian exiles. Vahan Terian (1885–1920), who was born in Tiflis (Tbilisi) and spent much of his short life in Moscow and St Petersburg, composed a poem about Ararat even though he confessed that he had never seen it. At a time when the Armenian people had experienced unspeakable horrors and been brought to the verge of total annihilation, Terian wrote:

> Luminous vision of pure light,
> shining with gleaming snow intact
> you are the refuge and the proof
> of the covenant and pact
> that our people will endure.
> Mist-endowed mystery, rampart
> of the sublime force,
> promise that the crucified will rise,
> refuge of dying man, Ararat,
> undying heart of our ashen land.[1]

Leafing through a collection of Biblical illuminations by the modern Armenian artist Lilit Amarjanyan, I came across a miniature that echoes Terian's imagery. Christ, radiant with light, is nailed to a cross set on a Golgotha placed between the two peaks of Ararat. In a note on her work the artist writes of a 'parallel symbolism' shared by the hill where Christ was crucified and 'Mount Ararat, symbolizing the shelter, survival, and resurrection of our righteous ancestor Noah and his generations'. Ararat, where God made his covenant with Noah, is seen both as a sign of the salvation of the Armenians and ultimately of all humanity. In front of Lilit Amarjanyan's three mountains is an enormous crowd of people representing, she says, 'redeemed mankind'.[2]

Triad
Three legends of Ararat

i) The disrespectful son

Moses Khorenatsi, often regarded as the father of Armenian historical writing, had a fondness for colourful legends. He tells of a king named Artashes, who ruled Armenia in the time of the Emperor Hadrian. Artashes died and a lavish funeral was arranged for him. His body was dressed in luxurious garments with a gold crown and placed in a golden coffin. A huge procession accompanied Artashes' remains to their burial place. His loving wives and concubines and devoted servants were apparently happy to kill themselves beside his tomb so that they could keep their king company in the afterlife. Witnesses were impressed. They said that the occasion showed that the Armenians were a civilized and not a barbarian people.

One individual, however, was angered by the expense and the slaughter. Artavazd, son and heir of Artashes, could see his inheritance melting away before his eyes. Looking at the costly coffin and the heaps of dead bodies, he turned to his father's corpse and accused Artashes of having taken Armenia with him to the grave, leaving nothing but ruins for his son to reign over. Some remarks, however, can penetrate beyond the grave. Artavazd heard his father's voice cursing him. The dead man warned that if the new king should ever go hunting on Masis (Ararat) he would be taken by spirits and disappear into the darkness, never to be seen again.

Artavazd was unimpressed by his dead father's threat. A few days later he went to hunt wild asses on the slopes of Mount Masis. As the new king rode up the mountain he was suddenly struck by an attack of vertigo. He fell from his horse and tumbled into a deep abyss. Artavazd vanished into the darkness, and, as his father had predicted, he was never seen again.

The old women who told the story to Moses Khorenatsi assured him that Artavazd was still alive, chained up in a cave somewhere deep beneath the mountain. Two dogs (perhaps the hunting dogs that he had taken with him on his ill-fated expedition) constantly gnawed away at the chains. The storytellers informed the historian that Artavazd's anger was now so great that, if he should ever escape, he would cause the most terrible destruction. Fortunately his chains were strengthened whenever a blacksmith struck his anvil. Moses Khorenatsi recorded that even in his own time (somewhere between the fifth and the eighth century – scholars argue endlessly about it) Armenian blacksmiths would still strike their anvils three or four times on the first day of the week to make sure that Artavazd would remain confined in his cave beneath Mount Ararat.

Another story picked up by Moses Khorenatsi said that Artavazd hadn't really been Artashes' son after all. He was a changeling. Artashes had upset the dragon women: the wives of the descendants of Azhdahak the Mede. They took revenge by stealing the king's son and putting a dev (an evil spirit) in his place. Moses

Khorenatsi, however, dismisses this possibility. He suggests that Artavazd had been insane from birth, and that his madness finally caught up with him.

ii) Looking for the ark

For centuries Armenians regarded climbing to the summit of Ararat as both impious and impossible. Noah and his family had come down from the top of the mountain to repopulate the earth, and ever since then it was forbidden to clamber up to those heights. This taboo was reinforced by a story about the holy Syrian bishop St Hagop of Nisibis. It has its origins in the fifth-century Armenian *Epic Histories*, composed by an unknown author (but formerly ascribed to the probably non-existent 'Pawstos of Byzantium'), though over the years the tale has grown in the telling.

There are some who claim that St Hagop was related to St Gregory the Illuminator, the extraordinary religious hero who converted Armenia to the Christian faith. The Syrian bishop was on his way to visit his cousin in Holy Etchmiadzin. When he caught sight of Ararat, Hagop was overcome by a desperate desire to climb the holy mountain and discover Noah's Ark. The ascent was extremely difficult and the saintly bishop became thirsty. He prostrated himself, bowing his head to the ground in prayer. Suddenly water gushed out from the rock. Hagop was able to quench his thirst, while the water continued to flow. Later generations would know it as St Hagop's Spring and attribute all kinds of wonderful properties to it – exactly like the *ffynhonnau* linked to our sixth-century Celtic saints in Wales.

Refreshed by this experience, Hagop began to climb again. The ascent got increasingly difficult and the elderly bishop felt more and more tired. In the end he could go no further. He lay down on a rocky ledge and went to sleep. God took pity on him and sent an angel, who called the holy man by name, waking him up. The messenger told Hagop that a bit of the wood from Noah's Ark had been placed next to the spot where the bishop had fallen asleep. Hagop should take it, but he shouldn't continue with his climb, as God had forbidden it. The holy man did as he was told. He found the wood, described by the *Epic Histories* as 'a board seemingly taken and sliced off with a hatchet from a large plank'.[3] Clutching this precious souvenir, Hagop started cheerfully back down the mountain.

The *Epic Histories* compare Hagop's descent from Ararat with his bit of wood to that of Moses from Mount Sinai, and suggest that the relic turned out to be a powerful preaching aid. Some storytellers claim that he gave it to his relative Gregory and that it has been kept in Holy Etchmiadzin ever since. Pilgrims who visit that centre of Armenian Christianity are still shown a seventeenth-century reliquary containing a fragment of wood that is said to be the one that the angel gave to Hagop as compensation for not reaching the top of the mountain. His story was used to deter many generations of would-be climbers of Ararat.

iii) The man who disappeared

Legends give way before hard-headed facts – and then sometimes those facts in their turn give way again to legend. In 1829 Professor Friedrich Parrot from the University of Dorpat (now Tartu in Estonia) arrived at Holy Etchmiadzin. He was leading a scientific expedition that intended to make a detailed study of Mount Ararat. The Catholicos of All Armenians was soon aware that the ancient taboo on climbing the mountain would in no way deter his distinguished visitor. So, despite his misgivings, he selected Khachatur Abovian, a twenty-year-old deacon who spoke fluent Armenian, Russian, Tatar (Azeri) and Persian, to act as guide and translator for Parrot's party. The professor was impressed by the new recruit, praising Abovian's 'earnest thirst after knowledge, his modesty, self-denial, and pious feelings ... his courage and his perseverance'.[4]

Despite these admirable qualities Abovian's position was an unenviable one. The Catholicos informed him that he would have to continue to wear his monastic garments ('three long and full robes', according to Parrot) throughout the climb. The young deacon would also not be allowed to relax his adherence to the Etchmiadzin community's strict rules on fasting. Abovian was painfully aware of the hostility of many of his monastic brethren. They regarded the expedition as sacrilegious and mocked the idea that its members would ever reach the summit of Ararat. Parrot and his companions proved them wrong. The ascent was difficult and they had to make several attempts to reach the peak. In the end they succeeded. The professor was able to record triumphantly that 'about a quarter past three on 27 of September (9 October) 1829, WE STOOD ON THE TOP OF ARARAT'.[5] The six men incorporated in that 'we' included Khachatur Abovian, the first Armenian to climb Armenia's sacred mountain.

A sign was needed to prove to the sceptics in Holy Etchmiadzin that the climbers had indeed scaled Ararat. Risking his life, Abovian dug a hole in the ice on a steep slope to the north-east of the summit and set up a cross there. He deliberately chose a place that would be visible from the plain. The deacon also filled a bottle with ice from the peak of the mountain, taking it back with him to present to the Catholicos. Sadly, neither the cross nor the holy water proved sufficient to convince many of Abovian's fellow monks of his achievement. After Parrot returned to Dorpat the young Armenian was persecuted and humiliated. Having asked to become a layman once again, Abovian was expelled from the Etchmiadzin community, excommunicated and left destitute.

Fortunately Professor Parrot had not forgotten his young protégé. He petitioned the Russian authorities and in 1830 the Tsar awarded Abovian a scholarship. This enabled him to go to Dorpat University, where he spent the next five years immersing himself in mainstream European culture. On returning from the Baltic, Khachatur Abovian became an innovative educator and an inspiring patriotic thinker and writer. He was responsible for turning colloquial Eastern Armenian into a modern literary language. His most influential work, not published until 1858, was *The Wounds of Armenia*, the first Armenian novel. In his preface to the book Abovian declared that 'the guardian of a nation is its language and faith. And if we were to lose them, woe unto us!'[6]

One morning in April 1848 Khachatur Abovian walked out of his house in Yerevan and was never seen again. The cause of his disappearance has been the subject of a great deal of speculation. One suggestion is that his Armenian nationalist activities had attracted the attention of the Tsarist secret police. They may have quietly kidnapped him and spirited him off to Siberia. Another theory (probably little more than malicious local gossip) is that he had been carrying on with a local Turkish woman. It is said that her husband, having found out about their affair, murdered Abovian and buried him in the garden. Others claim that the writer had become increasingly depressed and committed suicide. However, as Hrant Adjemian notes in his study of Armenia's first novelist, 'the only tangible reality of all that has been said about Abovian's end is that he left his house on 2 April 1848 never to return ...'[7]

As a result, Khachatur Abovian, the pupil of the hard-headed fact-collecting scientist Friedrich Parrot, becomes the subject of another Ararat legend. On my first visit to the Matenadaran, the library of precious manuscripts in Yerevan, our guide showed us the document signed by the Catholicos giving the young deacon Abovian a dispensation to climb the holy mountain. The modern Armenian poet Gevorg Emin suggested the possibility that the writer had vanished because he 'went up Mt. Ararat to find eternal peace in its pure snows'.[8] The young woman in the Matenadaran shared that theory, telling us how Armenia's heroic literary pioneer mysteriously disappeared forever, into the mists of the mountain that he had been the first Armenian to conquer.

Colophon
Mountains, blacksmiths, and vanished heroes

As a young research student, living in an attic in Aberystwyth, I had a poster of T. H. Parry-Williams' poem 'Hon' ('This') pinned to the wall above my bed. Many years later one of my daughters, studying for an exam, scribbled the same verses on a piece of paper.

She stuck them in a strategic place beneath the bookshelf in our vicarage's *tŷ bach*, and tried to memorise them each time she went there.

'*Hon*' has become seen as one of the classic expressions of Welsh identity. Parry-Williams begins his poem with an attempt to escape from all the posturing and overblown rhetoric about the apparently insignificant country in which he had so accidentally been born. He escapes from Aberystwyth and ends up at his birthplace in the shadow of Yr Wyddfa (Snowdon):

> There is Snowdon and her companions;
> there is the poverty and bareness of the land,
> there is the lake and the river and the crag; and,
> indeed,
>
> there is the house where I was born.
> But see, between earth and sky,
> voices and ghosts are all about the place.[9]

The sight of the mountain and the landscape and the place that is so full of personal and ancestral memories has a shattering impact on him: he realises that he is a part of Wales and Wales is a part of him, so that turning his back on his country is impossible:

> I'm beginning to feel a bit unsteady, and I tell you, it's as if I'm being overcome by some sort of weakness;
>
> and I feel the claws of Wales tearing at my breast ... God help me, I can't escape from this.[10]

Parry-Williams' Yr Wyddfa/Snowdon is the archetypal mountain for the Welsh, as Masis/Ararat is for Armenians. Yet, however significant Snowdon may be, there are two factors that make Ararat an even more important mountain. The first is its link with the whole of humanity through the story of Noah. Ararat/Masis is the place where the human race is said to have been given a second chance. This gives it an aura that is both sacred and universal. A thirteenth-century French traveller, who stopped for a few days at the foot of Mount Ararat, was told by an elderly Armenian that 'Nobody should ascend Masis, for it is the Mother of the World.'[11]

The other factor is the inaccessibility of Ararat to those who live in the Republic of Armenia. Even if the ancient taboo that prohibited climbing the mountain has disappeared, a present-day St Hagop, or even a Khachatur Abovian, would be prevented from making the ascent by harsh geopolitical reality. The border was agreed between Soviet Armenia and Turkey at a time when Lenin was wooing the Kemalist government. The Armenian holy mountain was allotted to the Turks. Pilgrims to Khor Virap, near the foot of Mount Ararat, can gaze across at it, but they soon become aware of the barbed wire, the watchtowers and the military vehicles that mark a border that remains closed, despite the efforts of recent diplomacy.

It does not require a leap of the imagination to be aware how we, as Welsh people, would feel if Yr Wyddfa was handed over to a hostile power and fenced off by its soldiers so that, although we could see it, we could never approach it. In one of his poems Gevorg Emin expresses the frustration felt by many Armenians as they contemplate their visible but unreachable sacred mountain:

> ... we are planted
> stones.

> I curse my own immobility
> Is it for nothing
> this is Ararat, I am an Armenian
> and we are apart.[12]

*   *   *

Albert Lewis (Albert Fronhaul or Albert *y Gof* to the people of Brechfa) was our village blacksmith, like his father and grandfather before him. 'These days people go to college and take courses and get diplomas to become blacksmiths,' he told me. 'I learnt my craft by watching my grandfather and father and helping them. I grew up with it.' He described how, in his grandfather's day, the blacksmith was held in great respect in the community. His skill was essential to its survival and prosperity, and his craft went back to the beginning of the Iron Age, long before Christianity, when Gofannon was the god of the *gofaint* (blacksmiths).

Yr *efail* (the forge) was next to Fronhaul, and some of the older men from the village would call in there for a chat with Albert, whenever he was shoeing horses. Albert was a wit, a storyteller and a passer-on of local traditions – someone always worth listening to. Now the *efail* is empty, the hammer no longer clinks on the anvil and the stories are no longer handed down to the generations to come. A unique strand of human civilization has vanished.

*Looking out onto the foothills of Mount Aragats from
the 11th-century church of Amberd*

*The newly consecrated and ordained Bishop Vahan and myself in front of
the Altar of Descent in Holy Etchmiadzin Cathedral. The Altar of
Descent is where Armenian tradition says the Risen Christ appeared to
St Gregory and touched the soil of Armenia – it is therefore the most
sacred place in Armenia and the place where every new bishop celebrates
his first Badarak (Liturgy).*

49

When out-buildings of the Gandzasar monastery were destroyed during a key battle in the Nagorno-Karabagh War of the 1990s, these khatchkars were found hidden beneath the rubble.

The 14th-century Church of the Mother of God at Noravank is one of the masterpieces of Armenian church architecture. It was the final work of the sculptor, painter and architect Momik, who is buried beside it. Tradition says that he fell to his death from the dome after completing it.

The monastery of Khor Virap where St Gregory the Illuminator was imprisoned for many years in a deep pit. Beyond the monastery is Mount Ararat, on the other side of the closed border between Armenia and Turkey.

Catholicos Karekin II greeting pilgrims to Holy Etchmiadzin, the centre of Armenian Christianity. He is accompanied by a group of Iranian Shi'ite Muslin scholars, paying a courtesy visit to Armenia.

Standing beside the grave of the Armenian freedom-fighter General Garegin Nzhdeh (1886–1957), at the remote church of Spitakavor among the hills of Vayots Dzor

The medieval Church of the Mother of God on the Lake Sevan peninsula, which was an island until the level of the water of the lake was lowered by Soviet hydro-electric projects. The church has the cross and dome shape characteristic of much Armenian ecclesiastical architecture.

Faces of Karabagh Armenian freedom-fighters killed in the Nagorno-Karabagh War of the early 1990s, one of them the artist who produced the drawings beneath the photographs. An exhibit from the Museum of Perished Azatmartiks in Stepanakert, the capital of Nagorno-Karabagh.

Goshavank monastery in Tavush province was founded by Mkhitar Gosh, in the late 12th century. It contains a beautiful 'lacy' khatchkar carved by the medieval master Poghos. Its famous library was burnt by the Mongols; the scorch-marks remain on the walls.

The tympanum above the entrance to one of the churches at Goshavank reflects the skill of the Armenian stone-carvers of the area during the medieval period.

The tomb of Catholicos Khoren I outside the Cathedral of Holy Etchmiadzin. Khoren was martyred during the Stalinist purges, his remains buried secretly by some courageous women. Later his body was reinterred at Holy Etchmiadzin with the traditional Armenian funeral rites.

In the hills of Tarush province, with the forest monastery of Haghartsin in the background – an area not unlike the hills and forests of Brechfa, where I spent almost twenty years of ministry

This Soviet tank played a crucial role in the capture of Shushi during the Nagorno-Karabagh War and is now preserved as a war memorial. It was captured from the Azeri forces and painted with a 'battle cross' to identify it as belonging to the Karabagh Armenian army.

A hermit's cell at the 7th-century monastery of Harichavank in Shirak Province. An earthquake has left it perched on top of a pillar of rock, separated by an abyss from the rest of the monastery.

These khatchkars mark the site of the University of Gladzor, which flourished in the hills of Vayots Dzor in the late 13th and early 14th centuries. The university produced theologians who defended the independence of the Armenian church.

This gateway at Holy Etchmiadzin was built to celebrate the 1700th anniversary of Christianity becoming the state religion of Armenia. It shows King Trdat greeting St Gregory the Illuminator in 301 AD.

The beautiful and remote Church of Spitakavor in the hills of Vayots Dzor was built in the early 14th century. On my way there I heard a cuckoo call – an unexpectedly familiar sound so many miles from home.

This is one of the slender, delicately-carved early seventeenth-century khatchkars, originally in the cemetery of Julfa (or Djugha) in Nakhchevan, preserved at Holy Etchmiadzin. The khatchkars left at Julfa were destroyed by the Azeri army in an act of deliberate cultural vandalism.

Over the centuries the hammering of Armenian blacksmiths kept the irate King Artavazd safely chained up beneath Mount Ararat. If that hammering should cease the maddened king would escape from his bonds and destroy Armenia. Perhaps Armenian blacksmiths still strike a few blows on their anvils on the first day of the week and thus, despite its many troubles, their country and their culture has managed to survive. Meanwhile, in almost all our Welsh villages, the anvils have either disappeared or are silent: a symbol of our own invisible equivalent of Artavazd inexorably destroying the ancient heart of our nation.

* * *

Some heroes are meant to vanish leaving no known burial place. Moses is an obvious Biblical example. In Welsh tradition two of our greatest warriors similarly disappear: King Arthur and Owain Glyndŵr. I was once rebuked by a Church of England clergyman for having described King Arthur as Welsh rather than English in one of my books. 'Who do you think he was fighting against, then?' I asked. An embarrassed silence followed.

Even if imaginative and commercially-minded monks managed to fake Arthur's grave at Glastonbury, the older belief is expressed in a line from '*Englynion y Beddau*' ['The Stanzas of the Graves'] in a famous medieval manuscript from Carmarthen, the town where I now live: '*anoeth bid bet y arthur*'.[13] This can either be translated as 'Arthur's grave is difficult to find in the world' or 'Arthur's grave is a wonder of the world'. The implication seems to be that Arthur's burial place is a mystery, and it reflected a widespread

Welsh folk belief that the hero was asleep (probably in a cave, possibly under Yr Wyddfa) and would one day return to help his people in their hour of need.

In the early fifteenth century there would be a similar uncertainty about the death and burial of Owain Glyndŵr, whose rebellion had briefly given substance to the dream of a united independent Wales. The legend that haunted the popular imagination told of an encounter between Owain and the abbot of Valle Crucis (*Abaty Glyn-y-Groes*). The latter had gone out in the early morning mist to say his prayers when he met the fugitive hero. Owain rebuked the cleric for getting up too early. The abbot replied that Owain himself had risen too early by a hundred years. From this grew the feeling that Owain (like Arthur before him) would one day return. He too was said to be sleeping with his warriors in a cave – perhaps one of those in which he had hidden during his years on the run. Stories would be told about shepherds who had accidentally stumbled across his hiding-place.

In Armenia a similar role was given to Pokr Mehr, the last of the wild heroes of Sassoun, whose exploits form a part of the national epic. This developed orally over many centuries and was first transcribed and published by Bishop Karekin Srvantzdiantz in the 1870s. Pokr Mehr and his horse disappeared into the Rock of Van and, so the legend goes, remain there. Each year on the feasts of the Transfiguration and the Ascension the rock opens and Pokr Mehr rides out on his horse, covering in an hour the distance that would take most riders forty days. However, when he moves on from rocky ground to an earthy surface it proves too soft to bear the horse and its rider, and so they return to the rock.

One day a shepherd walks past the Rock of Van on Ascension Day. It splits open and he glances in and sees a gigantic man who can only be Pokr Mehr. The shepherd asks him when he will finally leave his hiding-place, and receives the reply:

> If I come out of this place,
> The earth will not sustain me.
> I will not stay on earth
> While the world is wicked
> And the ground is false.
> When the wicked world is destroyed and rebuilt,
> When the wheat grows to the size of a rose-pod,
> When the barley grows to the size of a walnut,
> It is only then that
> I and my horse will be allowed to leave.[14]

Khachatur Abovian, like Arthur, Owain and Pokr Mehr, is a vanished hero who lends himself to legend. Perhaps a day will eventually come when Armenia and Ararat will be reunited. At that moment it would hardly be surprising to see the nineteenth-century Armenian mountaineer, novelist and patriot emerging from the mists of the holy mountain to greet his people once again.

Notes

1   *Coming to Terms: Selected Poems of Vahan Derian*, translated by Diana Der Hovanessian (New York: Ashod Press, 1991), p. 13. 'Derian' is the Western Armenian spelling of the Eastern Armenian 'Terian'.

2   Lilit Amarjanyan, *Armenian Miniatures: Biblical Illuminations XX-XXI cc.* (Yerevan: Mashtots Institute of Ancient Manuscripts – Matenadaran, 2007), pp. 40, 119.

3   *The Epic Histories Attributed to Pawstos Buzand* (*Buzandaran Patmutiwnk*), translated by Nina G. Garsoïan (Cambridge,

Massachusetts: Harvard University Press, 1989), p. 78.

4   Friedrich Parrot, *Journey to Ararat*, translated by W. D.Cooley (New York: Harper & Brothers, 1855), pp. 125–6.

5   Parrot, *Journey to Ararat*, p. 191.

6   Khachatur Abovyan, *The Preface to Wounds of Armenia: Lamentation of a Patriot*, translated by Vahé Baladouni and John Gery (Yerevan: Museum of Literature and Art, 2005), p. 39.

7   Hrant Adjemian, *Khatchadour Abovian et la Renaissance Littéraire en Arménie Orientale* (Antelias: Catholicossat Arménien de Cilicie, 1986), p. 60.

8   Gevorg Emin, *Seven Songs About Armenia* (Yerevan: Sovetakan Grogh Publishers, 1983), p. 273.

9   T. H. Parry-Williams, *Casgliad o Gerddi* (Llandysul: Gwasg Gomer, 1987), p. 119.

10 *Ibid.*

11 Hamlet Petrosyan, 'The Sacred Mountain' in *Armenian Folk Arts, Culture and Identity*, edited by Levon Abrahamian and Nancy Sweezy (Bloomington and Indianapolis: Indiana University Press, 2001), pp. 33-9 (p.37).

12 'Ararat' in *Anthology of Armenian Poetry*, translated and edited by Diana Der Hovanessian and Marzbed Margossian (New York: Columbia University Press, 1978), pp. 281-2.

13 A. O. H. Jarman, *Llyfr Du Caerfyrddin* (Cardiff: Gwasg Prifysgol Cymru, 1982), p. 41.

14 *David of Sassoun: The Armenian Folk Epic in Four Cycles – The Original Text*, translated by Artin K. Shalian (Athens, Ohio: Ohio University Press, 1964), pp. 370-1.

2

Light

A candle in the darkness

'When you go into an Armenian church you must always buy a candle and light it,' our guide remarked on my first visit to the country. The ancient churches of Armenia tend to be quite dark. Windows are high up and narrow. This was partly for defensive reasons: the church, with its solid walls, was a place where people would gather for prayer and safety when yet another invading army attacked their community. It also had a theological message. The light of the Holy Spirit descends from above.

The *Badarak* (the Armenian Liturgy) contains a prayer to the Holy Spirit, written by the tenth-century Armenian mystical poet St Grigor Narekatsi (Gregory of Narek). In his commentary on the *Badarak*, Bishop Vahan Hovhanessian, the genial and scholarly Primate of the Armenian Church in Britain and Ireland, describes it as a private prayer 'for the spiritual preparation of the celebrant himself'. It is followed by a curious instruction written in the first person: 'I shall again repeat the same order of speech, until confidence in the upward contemplation of light be wonderfully revealed, announcing and bringing the good news of peace from on high.'[1] I have never summoned up the courage to ask an Armenian priest if this rubric is strictly adhered to.

Whereas the celebrant of the *Badarak* is caught up 'in the upward contemplation of light', the ordinary worshipper expresses his or her faith by lighting a candle in the darkness. In most of the churches of Armenia there is, just inside the door, a desk where cheap yellow candles, or more expensive white ones, can be bought. This stimulus to prayer is also an important source of income for the church as a whole. The candles are lit and placed in a tray full of sand covered with water. The act of lighting a candle in a dark church touches something very deep within many people. For the Armenians, who have known so much darkness, it is a powerful symbol of hope, recalling words from the prologue to St John's Gospel: 'The light shines in the darkness, and the darkness has not overcome it.'

One Armenian author interprets the action as a request for guidance: 'Lighting a candle in the Church is a sign that we are willingly seeking God's light and wisdom in making decisions, and are ready to follow His guidance when we receive it and to prove our willingness through our way of life.'[2] My own motivation in lighting candles in churches all over Armenia has been rather different, which perhaps may reflect my non-Armenian religious background. For me the candles with which I have tried to stave off the darkness have been lit as prayers of intercession for family members or parishioners or friends who have found themselves in agonizing or impossible places. Within the economy of God's love I am sure that both approaches are valid.

Triad
The three churches of the illuminator

i) The pit of darkness
The Armenian Apostolic Church gets its name from

the tradition that it was founded by two of Jesus' apostles: St Thaddeus and St Bartholomew. Both were martyred in Armenia, but their witness sowed the seeds of Christianity in the land. However, the harvest would be brought about in the fourth century AD only through the mission of a third holy man, St Gregory the Illuminator (Grigor Lusavorich). Moses Khorenatsi, the early Armenian historian, records the belief that Gregory's father pitched his tent over the grave of the martyred St Thaddeus. That night the future Illuminator was conceived on the holy spot and 'received the grace of that same apostle, and having been begotten beside his grave he completed what was lacking in his spiritual labours.'[3] This providential coincidence linked the Illuminator to his martyred predecessor.

Anak, Gregory's father, was a man with a rather different mission. King Khosrov of Armenia, who was a Parthian, had inflicted a humiliating defeat on the Persian king. The latter was desperate to be revenged. He offered a huge reward to anyone who was willing to assassinate Khosrov. Anak, although he was a Parthian himself, volunteered to carry out the deed. He went to Armenia and wormed his way into Khosrov's affections. Then he killed him. The infuriated Armenians wiped out all of Anak's family except two infants. One of them was Gregory, whose nurse smuggled him out to safety in Cappadocia. There he was brought up as a Christian. Meanwhile the Persians had invaded Armenia, but Khosrov's son, Trdat, managed to escape to Roman territory. The Romans later restored him to his father's throne.

Gregory became one of Trdat's courtiers. He accompanied the king back to Armenia, presumably hoping to make up for the murder committed by his father. Trdat was a devout pagan. He ordered Gregory to present an offering to the goddess Anahit on his behalf. Gregory refused, saying that his Christian faith would not allow him to do so. The king, outraged by this disobedience, subjected the courtier to twelve extremely unpleasant tortures, which Agathangelos, who tells the story, recounts in disturbing and gruesome detail. A French writer describes these agonies as 'the pre-figuration of the destiny of Armenia'.[4]

Despite his appalling suffering, Gregory refused to deny his faith. The king began to feel more sympathetic towards his victim. However, another of his courtiers intervened to disclose that the man being tortured was in fact the son of Anak, the murderer of Trdat's father. The king's anger was reignited by this, and he ordered the prisoner to be 'taken to the acropolis of the city of Artashat and let down into the bottommost pit that was incredibly deep until he died there.'[5] The orders were duly carried out and Gregory disappeared into the pit of Khor Virap ('Deep Dungeon') in the royal fortress across the river from Mount Ararat.

Pilgrims and visitors to the monastery of Khor Virap are still shown Gregory's dungeon and encouraged to go down into it. I chickened out the first time that I went there, but on the second occasion Naira, my guide, insisted – and so I descended into the depths. The idea of being abandoned at the bottom of a deep, dark, narrow place touches something profound in the human psyche. An Old Testament scholar once told me how, as a child, he had nightmares in which he was Joseph, thrown into a pit by his jealous brothers and left there all alone. A

London Armenian, who had just returned from a pilgrimage to the Holy Land, remarked that most of the places that he had visited had made little or no impression on him. The one exception was the deep dungeon under the High Priest's house, where Jesus is said to have been confined after his arrest. The thought of his Lord's lonely suffering there had moved him to tears. I wondered if he had also, perhaps subconsciously, linked it to Gregory's imprisonment at Khor Virap.

King Trdat assumed that Gregory would not survive for long in the pit. Its air was foul and its floor was muddy and home to several poisonous snakes. However, the latter were apparently unwilling to harm the saint. Agathangelos tells us that a widow who lived in the royal fortress was ordered in a dream to bake a fresh loaf every day and give it to the prisoner. Presumably she also supplied him with water. It is usually suggested that she must have been a secret Christian. Somehow, with her help, Gregory managed to survive in his appalling dungeon for thirteen years.

The Roman Emperor Diocletian had begun to persecute Christians. A party of nuns, led by the Abbess Gayane, fled across the border to Armenia, hoping to find a safe refuge there. They included an extremely beautiful young woman named Hripsime. She was said to have attracted the attention of Diocletian himself. He had been furious when she spurned his advances. The refugee nuns eventually arrived at Vagharshapat, Trdat's capital. Unfortunately the Roman Emperor had found out about their escape and sent a message to his Armenian ally asking him to track them down.

The nuns were duly discovered and detained. King

Trdat ordered Hripsime to be brought before him. As soon as he saw her beauty he became as besotted with her as his Roman friend had been. The king attempted to rape his prisoner, but Hripsime succeeded in fighting him off. Agathangelos tells us that 'she, strengthened by the Holy Spirit, struggled like a beast and fought like a man. They fought from the third hour until the tenth and she vanquished the king who was renowned for his incredible strength.'[6]

Foiled and humiliated, the Armenian king now attempted to bully Abbess Gayane into persuading her protégée to submit to his desires. Instead of doing so, the older woman encouraged Hripsime to continue to resist him. This she did: 'she struck him, chased him and overcame him; she wore the king out, weakened him and felled him. She stripped the king naked of his clothes; she tore his robes and threw away his diadem, leaving him covered with shame.'[7] Then the courageous young nun ran away. Unfortunately a gang of the king's henchmen tracked Hripsime down and brutally killed her. Gayane and the other nuns were also slaughtered with hideous cruelty.

The king's savagery did not go unpunished. Trdat was just getting into his chariot to go hunting when he had a sudden seizure and started behaving bizarrely. Modern authors suggest that he was suffering from some form of lycanthropy. Agathangelos cited a Biblical parallel for his affliction: 'in the likeness of Nebuchadnezzar, king of Babylon, he lost his human nature for the likeness of wild pigs and went about like them and dwelt among them.'[8] Medieval Armenian artists regard his plight in very literal terms: several carved reliefs and manuscript miniatures show Trdat in his kingly robes with a wild boar's head and impressive tusks.

Then Princess Khosrovidukht, Trdat's sister, had a vision in which a man shining with light told her that the only way that her brother could be cured was by releasing Gregory from his dungeon. When she told the courtiers about this they laughed at her. Everyone assumed that the prisoner must have died many years before. However the vision was repeated five times. The angel added threatening suggestions about the disasters that would follow if his orders were not complied with. An Armenian was sent to the fortress of Artashat to investigate. To his amazement he discovered that Gregory had survived, and the holy man was duly hauled out of Khor Virap and dressed in clean clothes.

In 2001, when Armenia marked the 1700th anniversary of becoming the first Christian country, the celebration began with His Holiness Karekin II, the present Catholicos of All Armenians, climbing down into the pit at Khor Virap. He emerged from its depths carrying a lighted candle, as a symbol of the Light of Christ that St Gregory brought to the people of Armenia. The Catholicos took this light to the Cathedral of Holy Etchmiadzin. There 'representatives of all the branches of the Armenian Church lit their candles from the Light in order to relight the Light of Faith in all Armenian churches, large and small, spread all over the world'.[9] It was a powerful reflection of the way in which Gregory himself had brought light out of a darkness that had been unable to destroy him.

ii) The descent of the only-begotten

Like all Armenian churches, the Cathedral of Holy Etchmiadzin has a stage (bema) at the far end on which the altar is set. However, what makes this particular church unique is a second altar placed right in the centre of the building. Etchmiadzin means 'Where the Only-begotten descended', and this altar stands on the spot where, according to tradition, the Risen and Ascended Christ came down to touch the earth of Armenia, making it holy ground. Pilgrims queue up to kiss a cross and a Gospel book placed in front of this sacred spot. That act of reverence touched something deep inside me when I shared in it, and it must be even more moving and significant for an Armenian Christian.

Gregory the Illuminator, released from his dungeon, was brought to King Trdat. The king and his followers begged the holy man's forgiveness, and Gregory instructed them in the Christian faith. It was a lengthy process: Agathangelos tells us that it went on for sixty-five days. On the night before the sixty-sixth day Gregory was keeping vigil in the place that is now Holy Etchmiadzin. Suddenly he heard a sound like the crashing waves of the ocean. The vault of heaven opened above him and an angel called to him to look up towards what would be revealed to him.

Gregory saw Heaven itself and its uncreated light flowing down towards him filled with shining hosts of angels:

> And in the likeness of minute specks of dust which in the sunny springtime play in their myriads in the rays passing through windows or sky-lights, so too these hosts filled everything below with their light, and as the lights streamed forward so did the hosts with it.[10]

In the midst of all these angels was a tall and terrifying man with a huge golden hammer in his hand. He flew down like an eagle and struck the ground with it. Gregory saw four columns of fire, each rising up from a circular golden base with crosses of light above them. One was on the spot where the hammer hit the earth, while the others were in the places where Gayane, Hripsime and their fellow nuns had been martyred. Beyond the columns and the crosses were 'marvellous vaults fitted into each other'. 'Above this,' Agathangelos reports the Illuminator as saying, 'I saw a canopy of cloud, wonderfully and divinely constructed in the form of a dome'. The original angel messenger informed Gregory that the 'fearsome and splendid man' holding the golden hammer was 'the providence of God' – in other words Christ himself.[11] The Illuminator was told to build a Christian temple at the place of his vision, and three chapels on the sites of the nuns' martyrdom.

He duly did so – and his vision had a lasting influence on Armenian ecclesiastical architecture. Perhaps the most perfect of all Armenian churches in the simple beauty of its exterior is that which still shelters the shrine of St Hripsime. It was built in 618 by Catholicos Komitas on the site of earlier chapels, and reflects the way in which Gregory's revelation was interpreted as a dome set above the shape of the cross. A variety of architectural refinements are used in developing this idea, but the underlying pattern is present both in the Church of St Hripsime and in other characteristically Armenian churches. The symbolism is powerful. It suggests that through the cross (Christ's cross and our sharing in it) we can be raised up to Heaven.

Once the churches had been built in honour of the

martyrs, Gregory felt able to heal King Trdat:

> the king, while he was standing among the people with the appearance of a pig, suddenly trembled and threw off from his body the pig-like skin with its tusk-like teeth and snout-like face, and he cast off the skin with its pig-like hair. His face returned to its own form and his body became soft and young like that of a newly born infant; he was completely healed in all his limbs.[12]

The Illuminator then embarked on a campaign of destroying pagan temples and idols throughout Armenia and setting up crosses instead. Perhaps not surprisingly this was met with violent opposition in some places. King Trdat issued an edict requesting the Archbishop of Caesarea to ordain and consecrate Gregory as priest and bishop. He did so, and on his return from Byzantine territory the Illuminator held a mass baptism in the river Euphrates. King Trdat, Queen Ashkhen, Princess Khosrovidukht and 150,000 others were all received into the Christian faith.

According to Agathangelos that was only the start: during the week that followed over four million men, women and children were baptized. Armenia had become a Christian nation. The man who had been responsible for this dramatic transformation would be praised by an eighth-century Armenian bishop as the one 'who opened the gate of light, of the true knowledge of God, to us who had strayed into darkness and made us worthy to be heirs of the life eternal.'[13]

iii) The new cathedral

The bearded man in the photograph has a gentle, thoughtful expression, tinged with sadness. He wears the Ararat-shaped hood that indicates that he is a celibate Armenian priest. The small cross attached to it is a sign that he is in fact the spiritual head of all Armenians. The caption beneath the picture reads: 'Khoren I, last Catholicos of Etchmiadzin'.[14] The book that contains it was published in 1943. By that time Stalin's attitude to the Armenian Church had changed fairly dramatically. Hitler's invasion of Russia in 1941 had meant that the Soviet leader needed all the support he could find – even from those Christians whom he had formerly persecuted so savagely. Nevertheless, when the book appeared it still seemed that Khoren I might well have been the last Catholicos of All Armenians.

He had been elected Catholicos in 1932 at a time when the Armenian Church, like all Christian organisations in the Soviet Union, was facing pressure and persecution. Somehow Khoren hoped that he might be able to shepherd his flock safely through the dangers of the time. In 1934 he was interviewed by an American journalist, who described him as 'an honest, competent man, aware of his difficulties but able to cope with them'. The Catholicos told him that 'On the whole I have little cause for complaint. The Bolsheviks understand my position and I understand theirs.'[15] His words were no doubt carefully chosen, but as Stalin's purges worsened even the Armenian Catholicos was no longer safe. On the night of 5 April 1938 he was murdered in his residence by government agents. The official announcement said that he had suffered a heart attack. No funeral service was allowed. The Armenian Church has never been short of courageous women. Six of them, at great risk to themselves, smuggled his body away and buried it secretly in the grounds of St Gayane Church.

It was a dark time. It must have seemed for some that the light kindled by St Gregory the Illuminator was in danger of being extinguished forever on Armenian soil. Yet the church survived – and eventually Armenia became an independent republic. On 7 September 1996 the murdered Catholicos received his due recognition. His body was moved to the precincts of the Cathedral of Holy Etchmiadzin and re-buried, with a full funeral service, alongside his fellow Catholicoi. Last time I visited the Cathedral I stood quietly at the grave of this modern Christian martyr and said a prayer and asked his blessing.

The early years of Armenia's independence were not without acute economic and political difficulties. In 2001, however, the 1,700th anniversary of St Gregory's conversion of King Trdat gave Armenians a chance to celebrate their deep-rooted Christian heritage. A tall cross had been set up in Republic Square in Yerevan on the exact spot where Lenin's statue had stood not long before. Gas burners in the cross were lit, no doubt to recall that moment before Gregory's mass baptism of Armenians in the river Euphrates when 'a bright light appeared in the likeness of a shining pillar, and it stood over the waters of the river, and above it was the likeness of the Lord's cross'.[16]

An even more powerful and lasting symbol of the change that had taken place in the country was the building of the Cathedral of St Grigor Lusavorich in Yerevan. Armenian churches and cathedrals are normally quite small (which makes Welsh visitors feel very much at home in them). The new cathedral, however, was built to contain a congregation of 1,700 – one for each year since the conversion of Armenia. An English priest told me that it was 'like a modern French Roman Catholic cathedral' – a description that I found rather off-putting. As a result, although its domes were visible from my hotel window, I didn't bother to go there on my first visit to the capital. Instead I restricted my wanderings to older, more traditional Armenian churches.

On a later visit to Yerevan I got over this misplaced cultural snobbishness and ventured into the new cathedral. I expected it to be rather bleak and soulless in its spaciousness. I suppose that it might have been, were it not for the surprising number of people who were sitting in its pews, praying quietly. They were almost all young – between late teenage and early thirties. As it was quite early on a weekday morning, perhaps they had called in on the way to work or to classes or lectures. I recalled something that my guide had said to me the previous year, when we were lighting candles and saying a prayer in the beautifully restored cathedral at Shushi in Nagorno-Karabagh: 'After seventy years we are coming back to church.' I also remembered a remark by the Archbishop of Artsakh at dinner a few days before: 'Ours is a church of young people.'

At the entrance to the Cathedral of St Grigor Lusavorich is a shrine containing relics of the Illuminator. They were brought from Italy – having originally found their way there through the vicissitudes of Armenian history and the rather questionable activities of certain long since dead and forgotten clerics. Pope John Paul II brought them back as an ecumenical gesture of friendship when he visited Armenia during the 2001 celebrations. The shrine creates a link between the very modern (and yet distinctively Armenian) building and St Gregory's original mission. To an observer it soon becomes obvious that the relics provide a focus for fervent and heartfelt prayer. The light the Illuminator kindled so many centuries ago continues to burn brightly, despite many attempts to extinguish it along the way.

Colophon
Belonging, holy ground, and the patron saint

Perthyn is one of our key words in Welsh. We belong to a particular family and a particular place. '*Ydych chi'n perthyn?*' ('Are you related?') is a frequent question. As a young curate one of the best bits of advice that I was given by a kindly parishioner was '*Peidiwch â dweud dim byd am neb. Ry'n ni i gyd yn perthyn fel perfedd moch ffor' hyn!*' ('Don't say anything about anyone. We're all related like pigs' intestines around here!'). Relationship and place are intertwined. '*O ble 'dych chi'n dod?*' ('Where are you from?') is another common query. People are fitted into a map of the world and a broad family network.

Quietly listening in to their conversations in Cardiff and elsewhere, I've become aware that Armenians have a fairly similar approach to things, even though events (and sometimes quite unspeakable horrors) may have uprooted them from their ancestral area. They can work out that they are each other's third cousins twice removed in a way that would make anyone from a traditional Welsh community feel totally at home.

Until the comparatively recent explosion of

secularism in Wales there was a third strand to *perthyn*. People belonged to a religious community. They might be *eglwys* (church) or *capel* (chapel – of whatever denomination) but they all had a spiritual home somewhere. When I became rector of Llangeitho in rural Ceredigion in the early 1980s, my churchwarden, who was also the village shopkeeper, gave me a guided tour of the parish in his van. As we passed each house or farm entrance he would classify it according to the religious allegiance of those who lived there: '*Capel ... capel ... capel ... eglwys ... capel ... capel ... eglwys ... capel ...*' (*eglwyswyr* were very much a minority in that part of the world). Just occasionally he would point to a house where a newcomer from over the border had settled, remarking dismissively: '*Saeson – byth yn mynd i unman!*' ('English – never goes anywhere!').

Behind this religious element of *perthyn* are very deep and ancient roots. In the sixth century the tribes or extended families that were baptised by the saint who brought the Gospel to them, became a part of the *teulu* (family) of that saint. An element of this continuity persisted in some places in the closing decades of the twentieth century. I once told my congregation in the Carmarthenshire hill parish of Brechfa that the first Christians there had been baptised by St Teilo with water from the spring that became known as Ffynnon Deilo. They replied that all the church people who had lived in the village before the watercourse was blocked up by the Council in the 1960s had been baptised with water from Ffynnon Deilo too.

St Gregory the Illuminator provides the same sense of belonging and continuity for Armenian Christians.

The holy *muron* – the special chrism – that is used in Armenian baptisms is directly linked to that prepared by St Gregory himself. The relic of the saint's right arm, encased in gold, is used as part of the ceremony, in which the *muron* is prepared. Armenian Christians belong to the Illuminator's family: a relationship strengthened by the sense of sharing the faith he taught, and for which he suffered.

* * *

Since the time of the Emperor Constantine and his mother St Helena, Christian pilgrims to the Holy Land have deepened their devotion to their Incarnate Lord by visiting the most important places connected with his life on earth, literally attempting to walk in his footsteps. Among those pilgrims, from a very early period, were some from Armenia and others from Wales. Indeed it is probable that the first contact between Christians from the two countries occurred in Jerusalem.

The land of Armenia was sanctified by St Gregory. The central events of his life can be relived there, like those of Jesus in the Holy Land. The deep pit of Khor Virap helps Armenians to understand the Illuminator's suffering. The altar of descent in the Cathedral of Holy Etchmiadzin enables them to grasp something of his glorious vision and prepares them for their own encounter with the Risen Christ. Although our Welsh patron saint cannot claim anything to match the events of Khor Virap and Holy Etchmiadzin, the area around St David's contains his supposed birthplace, the scene of his baptism and many sites connected with his life and ministry. Both Holy Etchmiadzin and St David's Cathedral are among the world's most significant centres of Christian pilgrimage.

* * *

A country's patron saint enshrines the values that his or her people hold as precious. St Gregory the Illuminator is regarded as a martyr by Armenian religious writers. The tortures he suffered at the hands of King Trdat, and the long years he spent at the bottom of the dark pit, are seen as the equivalent of dying for the faith. His survival foreshadows the survival of the Armenian people themselves, repeatedly emerging into the light after periods of intense oppression and cruelty that might have been expected (and were sometimes intended) to wipe them out completely.

Light is at the heart of Armenian spirituality. The first Armenian expression that I learned was '*bari luys*' – the equivalent of our '*bore da*', except that '*luys*' literally means 'light' rather than 'morning'. St Nerses Shnorhali (1102–73) is one of the greatest Armenian mystical poets. He wrote a glorious *sharakan* (liturgical hymn), which he addressed to the uncreated heavenly light that can shine in the depths of our being as the light of dawn takes the darkness from our world:

> Light. Light, and source of all illumination,
> housed in unapproachable light.
> Heavenly Father, most blessed among the
> luminous, primordial light.
> In the dawning morning light, bring also
> the light of understanding into our souls.[17]

Shnorhali's prayer reflects the mission of the Illuminator: to bring that same divine light to the people of Armenia.

I once wrote a book about the sixth-century Welsh saints entitled *Candle in the Darkness*. In it I told how St David and his contemporaries also sought to bring light and hope to a society confused and anxious after the departure of the Romans and the invasions by Saxons, Picts and Irish. St David's last command to his followers, as recorded by the anonymous anchorite of Llanddewi Brefi, remains at the heart of Welsh Christianity and of our self-understanding as a nation: 'Lords, brothers and sisters, be joyful and keep your faith and your belief, and do the little things that you have heard and seen from me.'[18] A true patron saint, with God's help, gives a nation what it most needs. Both St Gregory the Illuminator of Armenia and St David of Wales undertook that task.

Notes

[1]   Vahan Hovhanessian, *Remembrance of the Lord: A Biblical Introduction, Historical Review and Contemporary Commentary on the Divine Liturgy of the Armenian Church (Badarak)* (New York: St Vartan Press, 2008), p. 80; *Divine Liturgy of the Armenian Apostolic Orthodox Church with Variables, Complete Rubrics and Commentary*, translated by Tiran Archbishop Nersoyan, revised fifth edition (London: Saint Sarkis Church, 1984), p. 35.

[2]   Dér Stépanos Dingilian, *A Spiritual Journey Through The Holy Badarak* (Glendora, California: The Author, 1998), p. 97.

[3]   Moses Khorenats'i, *History of the Armenians*, p. 221.

[4]   Luc-André Marcel, *Grégoire de Narek et l'Ancienne Poésie Arménienne* (Yerevan: Nahapet, 2005), p. 4.

[5]   Agathangelos, *History of the Armenians*, translated by R.W. Thomson (Albany: State University of New York Press, 1976), p. 135.

[6]   Agathangelos, *History*, pp. 189, 191.

[7]   Agathangelos, *History*, p. 199.

[8]   Agathangelos, *History*, p. 217.

[9]   Levon Abrahamian, *Armenian Identity in a Changing World* (Cosa Mesa, California: Mazda Publishers, 2005), pp. 133-4.

10   Agathangelos, *History*, p. 277.
11   Agathangelos, *History*, pp. 279, 283.
12   Agathangelos, *History*, pp. 311, 313.
13   Abraham Terian, *Patriotism and Piety in Armenian Christianity: The Early Panegyrics on Saint Gregory* (Crestwood New York: St Vladimir's Seminary Press and St Nersess Armenian Seminary, 2005), p. 162.
14   M. A. Navarian, *L'Église Apostolique Arménienne et sa Doctrine* (Paris: J. Vrin, 1943), p. 94.
15   Mary Kilbourne Matossian, *The Impact of Soviet Policies in Armenia* (Leiden: E.J. Brill, 1962), p. 150.
16   Agathangelos, *History*, pp. 367,369.
17   Hymn to the Light', Der Hovanessian and Margossian, *Anthology of Armenian Poetry*, pp. 66-7.
18   *The Welsh Life of St David*, edited by D. Simon Evans (Cardiff: University of Wales Press, 1988), p. 13.

3

Khatchkars

The true cross and the tree of life

The Matenadaran stands, appropriately enough, at the end of the long Yerevan boulevard named after St Mesrop Mashtots, the creator of the Armenian alphabet. This library of illuminated manuscripts is an impressive and beautiful building. Climbing up the steps towards it, I couldn't help glimpsing a remote but definite family resemblance to our own National Library of Wales in Aberystwyth, where I once spent three years collating not very good Anglo-Welsh poetry from seventeenth-century manuscripts.

The Matenadaran is clearly and proudly Armenian. At the foot of the steps is a monumental statue of Mesrop Mashtots himself, blessing Koriun, his young pupil and biographer. In front of the building are six more statues, commemorating the great figures of Armenian classical culture. The three that particularly caught my eye were of Davit Anhaght, Armenia's greatest philosopher, Mkhitar Gosh, who codified the Armenian laws and wrote fables that helped to convey their principles to ordinary people, and Frik, an angry poet who took God to task for the unfairness of the world that he had made – and who would probably have got on rather well with our own medieval Welsh-language poet Siôn Cent. A medieval *khatchkar*, or cross-stone, was set against a wall to the right-hand side of the Matenadaran courtyard. A party of lively schoolchildren were swarming up the steps and soon caught sight of it. '*Khatchkar! Khatchkar!*' they shouted out in joyful recognition and ran over to examine it. A couple of days later I bought myself an *Aybbenaran* (a primer or ABC book for children starting school) in the hope that it would help me as I wrestled with the complexities of Mesrop's alphabet. On page 31 there was a picture of a *khatchkar*. It was obviously something with which even the smallest children were familiar.

The *khatchkar* combines the Cross and the Tree of Life. It is a symbol of Christ's victory and resurrection. A French Armenian scholar has described it as 'one of the most potent symbols of the distance that separates Armenia from the Greek and Latin worlds'.[1] It differed from the painted icons of Byzantium and also from the crucifixes brought by the Roman Catholic missionaries who arrived in the wake of the Crusades. The number of medieval *khatchkars* that include the figure of the crucified Christ can almost be counted on the fingers of one hand. The Cross that is transformed into the Tree of Life has become a symbol of the distinctive character of Armenian Christianity.

A suggestion of its origin can be found on the lintel of an Armenian architectural masterpiece that now stands neglected just across the border in Turkey. The church at Mren was completed around 639–40 on the orders of two Armenian princes. One of them, Davit Saharuni, had helped the Byzantine Emperor to recover the True Cross, which had been stolen from Jerusalem by the Persians. It was brought back to the holy city in triumph in 630. In the *Armenian History* attributed to Bishop Sebeos there is a vivid description of the fervent and tearful reception that the sacred relic received there. The author tells us that 'No one was able to sing the Lord's chants from the fearful and agonizing emotion of the king and of the whole multitude.'[2]

The restoration of the True Cross was especially significant to Armenians for several reasons. St Gregory the Illuminator, the agent of Armenia's conversion, had set up crosses and was said to have told his followers that 'Only in front of this all saving sign should you worship the Lord God your creator.'[3] Armenian pilgrims had flocked to Jerusalem from the fourth century onwards and the True Cross had become the focus of the devotion of many of them. The involvement of a leading Armenian prince in its recovery was therefore particularly important for his fellow countrymen.

Davit Saharuni was determined to leave a lasting memorial to his achievement. The lintel over the north door of the church at Mren portrays, carved in relief, the Emperor Heraclius, who has just got down from his horse. He leans forward to receive the True Cross. It is presented to him by a kneeling Davit Saharuni, behind whom, holding a censer, stands Modestus, the Bishop of Jerusalem. On the far right, beyond the cleric, is a tree that Patrick Donabédian interprets as a palm tree. I can't help wondering if it doesn't in fact represent the Tree of Life, which would mean that the sculpted lintel contains the two elements that would later come together in the *khatchkar*.[4]

There is something poignant about this carving. By the time the lintel was installed Heraclius' brief triumph was over. The Arabs, fired by their conversion to Islam, had surged out of their peninsula overwhelming both Byzantines and Persians. Jerusalem was already in their hands, but the True Cross had been moved to safety in Constantinople.

Armenia itself was about to be threatened by this new invading force. Almost two and a half centuries would pass before the Arab hold began to weaken and Armenian Christian devotion to the Cross of Christ would re-assert itself with the appearance of the unique symbolism of the *khatchkar*.

Triad
Three types of khatchkar

i) The 'lacy' khatchkars of Momik and Poghos

We were standing in front of the two-storey Church of the Mother of God at Noravank, one of the most beautiful buildings in Armenia. Our guide told us that an architect had fallen in love with the daughter of an Armenian prince and asked for her hand in marriage. The prince replied that the architect could marry her only if he could build a church that was unlike any church that had ever been built before. The suitor did so, producing a flawless two-storey church. He was just about to put the cross on the dome to complete the building and claim his prize when he was given a shove by one of the prince's henchmen – and plummeted down to his death.

It's certainly true that Momik, the architect, is buried beside the church, having died just before its completion in 1339. However, I was not convinced by the guide's story. I smiled condescendingly. I had read that Momik was a *vardapet* – a learned monk who had taken a vow of celibacy. He would not have been allowed to marry his patron's daughter, even if he had wanted to do so. My smugness later received its comeuppance. One of the authors of a new monograph on Momik has pointed out that, even though he is described as *'vardpet'* on inscriptions, the word is no longer seen as an abbreviation of *vardapet*; 'now it is proved that the word *vardpet* means architect'.[5] He was, in fact, married, and the names of his son and grandson have been discovered.

Momik was also was an illuminator of manuscripts, a sculptor and the carver of some of the finest *khatchkars* ever produced. In a colophon to a manuscript he had begun illuminating in 1307, Momik reveals that he had had to abandon it for a time because of trouble with his eyesight. However he goes on to say that 'The light of my eyes returned to me in 1331, after many years, through my hope which was in Jesus ...'[6] He was thus able to write the colophon in the Gospel-book, which was being presented to the Church of the Mother of God at Noravank. This suggests to me that, if indeed the architect did fall from the dome of his unfinished church, it was probably the result of short-sightedness, rather than the treachery of his patron.

However, there is something rather unnerving in the discovery that Momik's brother, nephew and niece all died on the same day in 1333 – the year of the architect's own death. Karen Matevosyan comments that 'the dates make us suppose that in 1333 a disaster happened to this family. They could have died from an epidemic or an enemy attack ... Possibly, that unfortunate day Momik too was with them.'[7] The origin of the guide's folk tale may lie somewhere in this traumatic event.

One of the first rules of thumb given to those who become interested in *khatchkars* is that a simple design usually denotes an early date. Ninth- and tenth-century *khatchkars* tend to concentrate on the Cross, with branches of the Tree of Life growing out like wings from its base. Simplicity does not necessarily mean crudity. The ninth-century *khatchkar* from the monastery at Makenis, now at Holy Etchmiadzin, has an elegance that imprints itself on the memory.[8] As the centuries went by the carvings became increasingly elaborate, until by Momik's time they had reached the height of complexity.

Momik's masterpiece is a *khatchkar*, which is also preserved at Holy Etchmiadzin. He carved it at Noravank in 1308, a year after he started illuminating the manuscript, which he later had to set aside. It is a work of quite astonishing delicacy. The effect produced is that of lace – and it is almost impossible to believe that it is in fact carved stone. It is hardly surprising that Momik's eyesight was ruined by the concentration needed to produce such detailed carving.[9] I find the contrast between this 'lacy' *khatchkar* and the one that was put on Momik's grave beside the church at Noravank particularly fascinating. The latter is small and of a type that might have been produced several centuries before. Yet it is as perfect in its simplicity as the masterpiece he had carved for one of his patrons was in its complexity. His memorial reflects some the deep humility that seems to have been a characteristic of this extraordinary artist.

In his remarks about his eyesight Momik mentions that a *vardapet* named Poghos had been working with him on the Gospel-book. This Poghos shares a name with the other master of the 'lacy' *khatchkar*, and it is tempting to think that they were one and the same person. He carved his two most famous works for the monastery at Goshavank. One of them, produced in 1291, remains there. The other, from a slightly later date, is in a rather damaged condition and has been moved to the State Museum in Yerevan.

On my first visit to Goshavank my driver spoke enthusiastically about the faithfulness of the people there. 'They have not had a priest since Stalin's time,' he said, 'yet they still go to the church every Sunday to light their candles and pray. They deserve to have a priest.' Having spent almost twenty years as a Welsh country parson, I started to fantasize about moving to this remote corner of Armenia. Then reality kicked in. The Armenian *Badarak* (Liturgy) is very long and hugely complicated and requires a powerful singing voice, an instinctive ritual sense, and fluency in *grabar* (Classical Armenian). As I possessed none of these qualities, and wasn't even an Armenian, there was no way that God might be calling me to Goshavank.

Instead my mind began to focus on Poghos' astonishing *khatchkar*. The delicacy of his work led him to be nicknamed 'the embroiderer'. Some say the stone carver derived his patterns from traditional Armenian lace making, others that the lace-makers took their lead from Poghos. Whatever the truth of that may be, the result is remarkable. Almost as much of a miracle is the fact that, a century after its creation, it survived the burning of the monastery by Timur the Lame. The Goshavank 'lacy' *khatchkar* and its companion in the Museum in Yerevan are said to have been carved by Poghos in memory of his parents. It must rank as one of the most remarkable acts of filial piety in human history.

ii) Vahram's Khatchkars of the saviour

In 1031 the learned nobleman Grigor Magistros gave an unusual gift to an Armenian monastery. It was a carved wooden icon, showing Christ being taken down from the Cross by Nicodemus and Joseph of Arimathea. Above the figure of Christ was a dove (representing the Holy Spirit) and a hand pointing downwards (signifying God the Father), giving a Trinitarian element to the depiction.[10] Some experts have questioned the icon's provenance, suggesting that it may have originated in Georgia. What is certain is that the Armenians took it to their heart and it became an object of popular devotion. It can still be seen in Holy Etchmiadzin.

As has already been noted, *khatchkars* do not normally include the figure of the crucified Christ. This is because their imagery derives from the True Cross discovered in Jerusalem by the Emperor Constantine's mother, St Helena. *Khatchkars* focus on the Cross as a sign of victory, resurrection and redemption, rather than as a portrayal of Christ's suffering. The Armenians, after all, have had much more than their share of agony over the centuries. It is perhaps not surprising that they have preferred to depict the Cross as a sign of hope.

However, during the 1270s and 1280s something extraordinary happened. A sculptor named Vahram began to produce a series of *khatchkars* that became known as '*Amenaprkich*' or 'Saviour of All'. They show Christ on the Cross and seem to have been based on Grigor Magistros' wooden icon, though the figures of the Virgin Mary and St John the Evangelist have been added to the two disciples. One of the best-known examples is now at Holy Etchmiadzin, while another is in the famous monastery of Haghbat in northern Armenia.[11]

A suggestion sometimes made to explain Vahram's

radical and almost unique break with well-established Armenian tradition is the political situation at the time that the 'Saviour of All' *khatchkars* were produced. Greater Armenia, the area in which Vahram lived and worked, was under Mongol domination. Some of the Mongol khans, although shamanists themselves, had wives who were Nestorian Christians. They behaved leniently towards the monasteries in Armenia, often exempting them from taxes. They had also welcomed a diplomatic and military alliance with the Armenian Kingdom of Cilicia. By the second half of the thirteenth century it had become clear that the Mongol leaders were about to choose between Christianity and Islam. It is possible that Vahram produced his 'Saviour of All' depictions of Christ on the Cross to help persuade them to accept the Christian faith.

If that was his motive, it proved unsuccessful. By the end of the thirteenth century the Mongols had opted for Islam. The Christians of Armenia were discriminated against and faced poverty and starvation. Vahram's remarkable *khatchkars* survived, however, and were seen as a source of healing and a focus for pilgrimage and prayer.

In 2009 I visited a craft shop in Stepanakert, the capital of Nagorno-Karabagh. Many of the items there had been made by ex-soldiers disabled in the bitter war between Armenians and Azeris in the early 1990s. They had received training as wood carvers at the Rehabilitation Centre established in Stepanakert by Baroness Caroline Cox. Earlier I had been told the story of one such man who had been paralysed from the waist down as a result of being injured in battle. He had sunk into despair, taking to drink and maltreating his family. The Centre had rescued him, teaching him to carve wood and earn a living again. His self-respect had returned.

My eye was caught by an unusual wooden cross. It had the characteristic shape of the crosses carved on Armenian *khatchkars*, but skilfully inlaid in the wood was a figure of the crucified Christ. The man at the counter told me that it had been made by one of the ex-servicemen from the Centre. I bought it and showed it to an American-Armenian acquaintance. She was dismissive: 'It's not a proper Armenian cross at all. It's more like a Catholic crucifix.' I remembered the wood carver I had been told about. He may even have been the man who made this hybrid cross. Perhaps it expressed, through the suffering figure, the agony and despair that he had felt when he seemed worthless and a burden to himself and to everyone else. But then came new hope and resurrection – signified by the cross becoming an Armenian Tree of Life. It now hangs on the wall of the clergy vestry in our church in Carmarthen – and to me it echoes the message that Vahram once tried to teach the Mongol khans.

iii) The vanished Khatchkars of old Julfa

My second visit to the Cathedral of Holy Etchmiadzin coincided with the reception of a delegation of Shi'ite clerics from Iran by the Catholicos of All Armenians. Armenia is dependent on Iran for oil and many other goods, so the Church was making its contribution to good relations. While a crowd gathered outside the cathedral entrance to await the arrival of the Catholicos and his distinguished guests, I wandered off to look at Etchmiadzin's *khatchkars*, which include some of the finest examples in the world. One of them was particularly attractive. The slender stone had been carved with an elegance of design that emphasized the Oriental element in Armenian art. Naira, my guide, told me that the *khatchkar* had come from Old Julfa in Nakhichevan, which, since Soviet times, has been an enclave officially attached to Azerbaijan, but separated from it by strip of Armenian territory.

At the beginning of the seventeenth century Julfa was a prosperous commercial centre on the Silk Road connecting China with the Levant. One Armenian poet even claimed that it 'surpassed Paris of the French'.[12] When Shah Abbas, the powerful ruler of Iran, visited their town, the people of Julfa decided to welcome him in suitable fashion. He was met by a procession of the inhabitants dressed in splendid robes made of golden cloth. They escorted the Shah along a path covered with carpets and fine-woven cloth to the house of one of Julfa's leading merchants. There the potentate was presented with a tray laden with gold coins.

It was a disastrous mistake by the Julfans. The Shah was certainly impressed by their ostentatious display of opulence. He decided that such successful entrepreneurs belonged at the heart of his empire rather than on its fringes, and that their skills could be used to ensure that Iran would dominate the silk trade. In the winter of 1604–5 he forcibly and brutally deported the people of Julfa. Many of them died during the terrible journey. The survivors were settled in New Julfa, a suburb of Isfahan, where they resumed their position in the silk trade, and built several magnificent Armenian churches.

They left behind (in what now became known as 'Old Julfa') an enormous cemetery containing a remarkable number of *khatchkars*. The art of Armenian stone-carving in Julfa had undergone a renaissance in the town, fuelled by the prosperity of its inhabitants. A particular style was developed by its gifted sculptors, producing masterpieces like the one that I noticed in Etchmiadzin.[13] In 1648 a traveller recorded that there were about 10,000 well-preserved *khatchkars* in the cemetery at Old Julfa. Towards the end of the nineteenth century the number was drastically reduced when contractors building a railway broke up thousands of the carved stones to use as rubble. Even so, in 1903–4 there were still 5,000 left. By 1915 the number was down to 2,300, while in 1990 Ayvazian recorded about 2,000, some of them in a state of disrepair.

Now there are none left – apart from the few that had been moved to safety earlier, like the example in the courtyard of Holy Etchmiadzin. The Nagorno-Karabagh conflict of the early 1990s left the Azeris with a legacy of bitterness towards Armenia and its heritage. Although an attempt by the authorities to bulldoze the cemetery and its *khatchkars* in 1998 was halted by UNESCO, between 2002 and 2005 Azeri soldiers cleared away all the carved stones, smashed them to pieces, and dumped them in the river Arax. The army of Azerbaijan has now converted the site of the cemetery into a firing-range.

In 2004 the Armenian artist Ararat Sarkissian, moved by the loss of the Old Julfa *khatchkars*, produced a collection of oil prints of *khatchkar* designs on handmade paper. A year later these appeared as a book from a Yerevan publishing house.[14] A paper *khatchkar* ('cross-stone') might seem to be a contradiction in terms. However, the artist's work brings home the message that these ancient masterpieces of art and piety, however solid and permanent they may seem, can be very easily destroyed by those who want to obliterate the cultural and religious heritage of which they form a part.

Colophon
The true cross, the Celtic cross, and cultural obliteration

Armenians are sometimes called 'the People of the Cross', both on account of their devotion to the sign of Christ's Passion and because of their suffering for their faith over the centuries. The Cross also has a central place in Welsh spirituality. An illustration would be the Good Friday customs in Brechfa, when I was rector there. The young people of the church would give a dramatic reading of Y *Groglith* – the account of Christ's Passion from St John's Gospel that gives the day its Welsh name: *Dydd Gwener y Groglith*. Then one of them would pick up the simple rough-hewn cross that had been placed on the altar. It would be carried through the village to the farmyard at Maes-y-groes ('the Field of the Cross'). There, at the place where the merciless Lords of the Forest of Glyn Cothi were said to have executed their victims in Elizabethan times, an open-air service would be held. It would begin with a hymn by William Williams, Pantycelyn, Carmarthenshire's great eighteenth-century hymn-writer:

> The blood of your Cross that raises up
> the weak as a great conqueror;
> the blood of your Cross
> that humbles a host of strong giants;
> let me feel

a breeze from Calvary's hill.[15]

Davit Saharuni may have given the Armenians their special link with the True Cross when he helped restore it to Jerusalem. The Welsh claimed an even stronger connection with this powerful relic. In the early Middle Ages they developed an unshakeable belief that St Helena, the mother of the Emperor Constantine and the discoverer of the True Cross, was originally a Welsh princess. This theory is dismissed by modern historians, who insist that she was in fact a tavern-keeper's daughter from what is now Romania. Nevertheless our Roman roads in Wales are still called *Sarn Helen* ('Helen's Causeway'), after Constantine's mother.

The most significant reliquary in medieval Wales was the *Croes Naid* ('Cross of Destiny'), which was carefully guarded by the Princes of Gwynedd for centuries. Covered with fine jewels, it was said to contain a fragment of the True Cross. It fell into the hands of the English after the death of the last native Prince of Wales, and was paraded through the streets of London before being taken by Edward I on his Scottish campaign. It seems to have disappeared after 1353, though there have been attempts to claim it back from the English in recent years.

* * *

The 'Abraham Stone' at St David's Cathedral is the gravestone of the sons of Bishop Abraham, who was killed by Viking raiders in 1080.[16] It contains one of the most iconic Welsh forms of the Celtic cross, which formed the basis of the design of the cover of the 1984 Church in Wales *Book of Common Prayer/Llyfr Gweddi*

Gyffredin. Since that book has been the basic of my daily prayers for over a quarter of a century, that particular version of the Cross is indelibly printed on my mind. It was therefore quite a surprise to come across an Armenian miniature from a manuscript illuminated in Artsakh (Nagorno-Karabagh) in the thirteenth or fourteenth century that contains a cross that is remarkably similar to the one carved in St David's a couple of hundred years before.

The miniature depicts the Last Supper. Jesus is seated in front of a round table. The heads of eleven of his apostles form a circle around it. Judas, the twelfth apostle, is disappearing into the lower right-hand border of the picture, on his way to betray his Lord. The design, which seems to mimic the Celtic cross on the Abraham stone, takes up the whole of the table. An expert on Armenian illuminated manuscripts remarks that 'The large ornate cross on the table, represented instead of the usual viands, symbolizes the Sacrifice of Christ'.[17]

Armenians get around. In the middle of the eleventh century, according to an early Icelandic historian, three Armenian bishops landed in his country. They were called Peter, Abraham and Stephen, and had apparently been invited there by the Norwegian king. This was only a few decades before the Abraham Stone was carved. If Armenian bishops could get to Iceland, might not an Armenian stone carver have reached St David's? It's an intriguing thought – but it seems far more probable that the apparent similarity between the monument in the west Wales cathedral and the miniature from Artsakh in the Matenadaran are merely a happy coincidence.

The possibility of an Armenian influence on the

development of the carved crosses that are a feature of the Celtic-speaking lands has been argued about by scholars for many years. Recently, however, they seem to have reached a consensus. *Khatchkars* and Celtic crosses are now generally seen as parallel developments on the Eastern and Western fringes of Christendom. Jacob Ghazarian, writing of Ireland and Armenia, speaks of striking artistic similarities between the stone crosses of the two countries, remarking that the two early Christian cultures 'were nourished through a common spiritual umbilical cord'.[18] Perhaps Hilary Richardson puts it best when she refers to 'a common underlying stratum of culture ... a culture that was preserved among Christian communities at great distances from each other and that linked their ways of thinking; and a culture that went far back to the victory of the faith and early celebrations of the Triumph of the Cross'.[19]

* * *

Cultural vandalism is a crime against humanity. On the slopes planted by the Forestry Commission above Cwm Cothi in Carmarthenshire is a prehistoric cromlech known locally as '*Bedd y Tywysog*' or 'The Prince's Grave'. When the neat ranks of conifers were originally planned it was decided that this ancient lump of rock would disrupt their tidiness. Orders were given for it to be dynamited and blown to smithereens. The forestry workers, many of whom had been brought up in the area, refused to carry out this task. Instead they allowed the rows of trees to bulge a little, preserving and protecting the grave that had been regarded as a special and sacred place for longer than anyone could remember.

Seeing a film of the callous destruction by Azeri soldiers of the slender, beautifully sculpted *khatchkars* in the cemetery of Old Julfa, my mind went back to the cromlech above Cwm Cothi. To the officials who gave instructions to obliterate '*Bedd y Tywysog*', the prehistoric burial place meant nothing. To the forestry workers it was a sign of their ancient roots there, and they were willing to risk punishment or dismissal to ensure that it survived. They proved to be more civilized than their ignorant or indifferent superiors.

The situation in Old Julfa was far more sinister. There the *khatchkars* were destroyed deliberately and even with enthusiasm. The aim of those who gave the orders, and of the soldiers who carried them out, was to obliterate a culture. They were trying to create the impression that no Armenians had ever lived in that part of Nakhichevan, producing elegant works of art that reflected their skill and their piety. Fortunately the *khatchkar* from Old Julfa preserved at Holy Etchmiadzin continues to give the lie to that barbarous and shameful claim.

Notes

[1] Patrick Donabédian, 'Le khatchkar, un art emblématique de la spécificité arménienne' in *L'Église arménienne entre Grecs et Latins*, edited by Isabelle Augé and Gérard Dédéyan (Paris: Guethner, 2009), pp. 151–67 (p.151)

[2] *The Armenian History attributed to Sebeos*, translated by R. W. Thomson, 2 vols (Liverpool: Liverpool University Press, 1999), I, 90.

[3] Agathangelos, *History*, p. 309.

[4] For pictures of the lintel see Patrick Donabédian, *L'âge d'or de l'architecture arménienne: VIIe siècle* (Marseilles: Éditions Parenthèses, 2008), p. 109 (fig. 167) and Jean-Michel Thierry and Patrick Donabédian, *Armenian Art* (New York: Harry N. Abrams, 1989), p. 366 (fig.202).

5   Karen Matevosyan and Lilit Zakarian, *Miniaturist Momik* (Yerevan: Nairi, 2010), p. 6, n. 13.

6   Quoted in Thomas F. Mathews and Avedis K. Sanjian, *Armenian Gospel Iconography: The Tradition of the Glajor Gospel* (Washington, D.C.: Dumbarton Oaks Research Library and Collection, 1991), p. 69.

7   Matevosyan and Zakarian, *Miniaturist Momik*, pp. 11–12.

8   See Thierry and Donabédian, *Armenian Art*, p. 160 (pl. 67).

9   See Levon Azarian, *Armenian Khatchkars* (Etchmiadzin: Holy See of Etchmiadzin and Calouste Gulbenkian Foundation, 1973), [pp. 110–12] (figs. 89–91) and Levon Azarian, *Khatchkar*, second edition (Milan, Edizioni Ares, 1970), p. 48 (fig. 46).

10 See Thierry and Donabédian, *Armenian Art*, p. 389 (fig. 292).

11 See Azarian, *Armenian Khatchkars*, pp.[98–101] (figs. 76–9), [106–7] (figs. 85–6); Thierry and Donabédian, *Armenian Art*, p. 408 (figs. 361 and 363); Sirarpie Der Nersessian, *Armenian Art* (New York: Thames and Hudson, 1978), p. 204 (fig. 157).

12 Hovhannes of Maku, quoted in Argam Ayvazian, *The Historical Monuments of Nakhichevan* (Detroit: Wayne State University Press, 1990), p. 62.

13 For examples see Thierry and Donabédian, *Armenian Art*, pp. 434–5 (figs. 484–92) and Azarian, *Khatchkar*, pp. 54–7 (figs. 54–7 – the Old Julfa khatchkar preserved at Holy Etchmiadzin is shown in figs. 56–7).

14 Ararat Sarkissian, *paper/Cross/stone* (Yerevan: Tigran Mets Publishing House, 2005).

15 *Emynau'r Eglwys*, third edition (Cardiff: Western Mail & Echo Ltd, 1956), p. 366.

16 See Wyn Evans and Roger Worsley, *Eglwys Gadeiriol Tyddewi 1181-1981 St Davids Cathedral* (St Davids: Gwasg yr Oriel Fach, 1981), p. 148.

17 Emma Khorkhmazian, Irina Drampian and Gravard Hakopian, *Armenian Miniatures of the 13th and 14th centuries from the Matenadaran Collection, Yerevan* (Leningrad: Aurora Art Publishers, 1984), [p. 111], note on pl. 69.

18 Jacob G. Ghazarian, *The Mediterranean Legacy in Early Celtic Christianity: A journey from Armenia to Ireland* (London: Bennett & Bloom, 2006), pp. 154–5.

19 Hilary Richardson, "Hands On' Dvin: Reflections on the Dvin Capital' in *Between Paris and Fresno: Armenian Studies in Honor of Dickran Kouymjian*, edited by Barlow Der Mugrdechian (Costa Mesa, California: Mazda Publishers, 2008), pp. 27–37 (p. 36).

4

Doves

The wings of a dove

The stout sheep looked distinctly fed up. Its owner had attached it to a bit of rope, which he held in one hand, while the other clutched a plastic bag of salt. A priest stood at the large stone slab in front of St Gayane Church in Holy Etchmiadzin. He was blessing salt that a large man was about to feed to a chicken. The chicken and later the sheep were about to be become *matagh* – a sacrificial Armenian thanksgiving meal. It was hardly surprising that the sheep looked so disconsolate. It tore a mouthful of grass from the church lawn: the 'hearty breakfast' of the condemned.

No doubt *matagh* originated in pre-Christian times, but by now it has acquired a respectable Scriptural pedigree. There is the ram in the thicket that God supplied to Abraham as a sacrificial substitute for Isaac. In the Armenian Bible and Armenian religious art, the thicket becomes a two-branched sabek tree, which prefigures the Cross of Calvary.[1] There is also the *agape* or 'love-feast' of the early Christians. *Matagh* is not intended to be an exercise in self-indulgence. The meal is an act of thanksgiving to God for a blessing of some kind: the birth of a child, surviving an operation or an accident, passing an exam ... The food is to be shared with the poor.

An old man was sitting near the entrance to the church enclosure with a cage full of doves. 'Are they meant to be sacrificed too?' I asked, feeling slightly queasy. 'No,' our guide replied. 'You can buy one for a thousand *drams* and let it go, saying a prayer or making a wish as you do so.' My youngest daughter was in hospital in Cardiff, and it suddenly seemed very far away. I fished out a banknote and handed it over. As I held the bird I could feel its heart beating. I whispered my prayer before letting the dove go. It flew up and away towards the snowy peaks of Ararat, like Noah's dove before it. Later I discovered that it would have been trained to return to the old chap by the gate, but that didn't spoil the sense of having offered up a heartfelt prayer in an unforgettable way.

Some days later we visited the extraordinary monastery of Geghard, hollowed out of the rock. It has a multitude of beautifully carved *khatchkars*, but there was one in particular that caught my attention. It stands to the right of the altar platform in the innermost church. Although there are a great many photographs of Geghard, I have never been able to find one of this particular stone – and I was glad to have the opportunity the following year to go back there and confirm that I hadn't imagined it. Instead of the foliage that sprouts from the foot of the Cross in most khatchkars, the sculptor has depicted two doves: signs of the Holy Spirit or emblems of hope and peace flying towards Mount Ararat.

Triad
Three keepers of doves

i) 'The monastery of doves'
Sometimes a story grips your imagination in such a way that you can't help repeating it. Robert the driver steered us along the road around Lake Sevan, Armenia's turquoise inland sea, as I chatted with

Naira, my cheerful and knowledgeable guide and translator. There were huts along the roadside, with young fishermen standing outside them. Each stretched his arms out wide exaggerating the size and the magnificence of the fish that he had caught in the lake and hoped to sell to us. The day before, we had visited the churches on the Sevan Peninsula. It had been an island until Stalin's hydro-electric schemes lowered the level of the lake. In the Middle Ages badly-behaved monks had been banished to the monastery there as a punishment. In Gostan Zarian's brilliant novel about Armenia during the days of the First Republic (1918–20), *The Boat on the Mountain*, he describes how enemies of the regime were interned there. I wanted to know if the churches on the peninsula were the ones referred to by Hovhannes Tumanian, one of the greatest Eastern Armenian writers, in a poem called 'The Monastery of Doves', which was adapted by Mischa Kudian for his collection of Armenian folk tales, *Three Apples fell from Heaven*. So I retold the story, as far as I remembered it.

It came from the time when Timur the Lame was devastating Armenia, causing terror and misery and taking thousands of prisoners. The brutal invader and his warriors stopped to rest on the shores of Lake Sevan. A hermit lived in a monastery nearby. Father Ohan was an ancient man with a flowing white beard. He had devoted his life to praying for his fellow Armenians. Now he was angry with God for allowing Timur to inflict such appalling suffering on his people. He left his church and came down to the lakeside, arguing furiously with the Almighty. Having reached the water's edge, he kept on going. As he walked across the water he continued to tell God exactly what he thought of him for callously abandoning his faithful Armenians.

Years later I came across another version of the story in which Ohan is called Father Hovhan. In this variant he walks across the waves, not because he is too busy disputing with God to notice where he is going, but simply to get away from Timur. He is able to perform the miracle because he has a wooden cross tied to his back, containing a fragment of the True Cross used to crucify Christ. Timur calls him back and promises him immunity for his monastery. Legends grow and change shape according to the taste and mood of the teller.

In the version that I tried to repeat to Naira and Robert, Timur promises the old hermit anything that he wants: wealth, glory or power. The holy monk dismisses the offer contemptuously, replying that his only wish is for the tyrant to release all his Armenian prisoners. The warrior chieftain is uncertain about this, and decides on a compromise. He tells Father Ohan that he is willing to release as many prisoners as can fit in the old man's monastery, on condition that the hermit prays for him.

Father Ohan agrees. Timur orders his warriors to allow their captives to follow the holy man into the monastery. They do so. The building is quite small. A hundred thousand Armenian prisoners pass through the door and still there seems to be room for more. Timur is startled by this, but since he has given his word, he orders his guards to keep on sending the prisoners in. Soon the number set free is over a million – but still the warrior chieftain refuses to intervene. Finally there are no more prisoners left. Timur is completely bewildered. He commands his men to go into the monastery and investigate. When they burst through the door they find only a handful of men inside. Father Ohan is kneeling in prayer. As he prays, the last remaining prisoners, like the others before them, are transformed by God's will into doves, and fly across the lake to the safety of the mountains beyond.

Naira knew the legend, of course. She told me that the 'Monastery of Doves' wasn't the one on the Sevan Peninsula. She looked thoughtful for moment. 'It's not on our itinerary,' she said, 'but I think we could manage a slight detour.' She and Robert had a brief discussion in Armenian, and a few minutes later we found ourselves at the foot of a rocky hill overlooking the lake. Passing some fine *khatchkars*, we climbed up to the simple monastery church of Hayrivank, which, tradition says, was Father Ohan's legendary 'Monastery of Doves'. After looking inside I wandered out to gaze across Lake Sevan to the mist-shrouded mountains on the other side. I thought of the terror that savage Timur and his merciless warriors must have caused to the people of the lakeside. I imagined the fishermen and their families crowded into the monastery, joining the monks in chanting '*Der Voghormya*' ('Lord have mercy'), that prayer from the heart uttered by Armenians across the centuries. Was there a miracle? If not, the horror that must have overwhelmed them was too unspeakable to imagine.

An image came to mind from one of the most remarkable works of early Armenian theology: a catechism traditionally attributed to St Gregory the Illuminator but more probably written by St Mesrop Mashtots, inventor of the Armenian alphabet at the beginning of the fifth century. The author writes of the faithful: 'Those who stand in this loyalty to the command of righteousness will take the form of a dove with rapid wings and will fly on the wings of the Holy Spirit to attain the kingdom of heaven, for which the saints remain yearning on earth ... They will be joined to the band of Christ, flying the swift flight of shining-feathered white doves, who have taken and represented in themselves the form of the Son of God who appeared to them.'[2]

Perhaps that was the true meaning of the legend of the 'Monastery of Doves'. After all, the cruelty of Timur the Lame and his warriors had left an indelible scar on the people of Armenia. They were aware that he was incapable of mercy. In 1389 the scribe Karapet of Aghtamar recorded the horrors which Timur's horsemen inflicted on the Armenian Christians living around Lake Van:

> They put the wondrous bishops to the sword; they ground the heads of the pious priests between stones; they cast the flock of Christ as food for the dogs; they trampled the children with their horses; they debauched the women, and carried off their infants into captivity. Like the threshing-floor of flails, they thrashed the children with their horses; and, in place of grain, rivers of blood began to spring forth, and in place of straw the bones flowed forth like dust.[3]

In the face of such brutality the only hope could be a transcendental one: that the souls of those slaughtered so savagely might rise like doves to heaven, while their bodies remained crushed on the rocks and earth of their homeland.

ii) The guardian of Harichavank

Artik is a rather depressing place in the northern Armenian province of Shirak. It was built as a new town during the Stalinist area. The family of one of the hapless French Armenian immigrants who were persuaded to settle in Armenia just after the Second World War was sent to Artik, and she expressed a desire to join them there. 'It's like Siberia,' a friendly Armenian lorry-driver warned her.[4] Ironically Artik's quarries produce the attractive pastel-shaded tuff stone that is used to construct all the most beautiful buildings in the country. Beyond this dreary town a road leads to the village of Harich.

It peters out in front of a complex of buildings, one of which was, in pre-Soviet times, a residence of the Catholicos of All Armenians. The leader of the Armenian Church would retreat there in summer, abandoning the scorching heat of Holy Etchmiadzin. Harichavank (*vank* is Armenian for monastery) might be Siberia-like in winter, but in the middle of the year it has a very pleasant climate. There was also a seminary, which was closed under the Communist regime. The great Armenian composer and collector of folk music, Komitas *vardapet*, had studied there. The gems of Harichavank, however, are its two churches, one built in the seventh century and the other added in 1201.

In May 2008, almost two decades after the collapse of the Soviet system, neither the Catholicos nor the seminarians had found their way back to this haunt of their predecessors. There was no sign even of a priest there. Instead there was an extraordinary old layman who had taken upon himself the task of looking after this ancient holy site and ensuring that it was still a place of prayer. He had very few teeth and his rather pungent clothes were full of holes. If I had met him in Carmarthen I would have assumed that he was sleeping rough and probably had a drink problem. Appearances, however, mean very little. It didn't take long for me to discover that I was in the presence of a mystic, perhaps even a saint: an unselfconscious holy man who would have been quite at home with the Desert Fathers of Egypt and Palestine, or St David and his followers in west Wales.

He loved the churches in his care. We wandered around examining their exterior. The old man enthusiastically pointed out the significance of the various Christian symbols carved on the walls. Suzy, my guide, a somewhat secular young woman from Yerevan, was clearly a bit embarrassed at having to translate all this religious stuff. As the caretaker moved on to reveal his next marvel, she whispered to me that 'people rather liked that sort of thing in Armenia in the Middle Ages.' We went into the Church of the Mother of God. It was filled with doves. 'They are signs of the presence of the Holy Spirit,' the old man explained, his eyes shining with joy. Stalin might have succeeded in removing the Catholicos and the priests and seminarians from Harichavank, but the doves remained.

We walked over to a room in the abandoned seminary. The caretaker had turned it into his own personal prayer room. Home-made shrines helped to sustain Armenian folk Christianity through the Communist era, and continue to enrich it now. The focus of the old man's devotional space was a medieval stone carving of a dove, in front of which he had many small yellow candles of the type that worshippers and visitors purchase and light on entering an Armenian church. The fine sculpture reminded me of the golden dove-shaped containers from which the holy *muron* – the special chrism blessed by the Catholicos every seven years – is poured at Armenian baptisms. Both stone and metal doves are as much symbols of the Holy Spirit as the birds in the Church of the Mother of God. Standing in front of the caretaker's treasured carving, we solemnly lit our candles and he spoke to God in Armenian and I spoke to God in Welsh.

iii) Hrant Dink

Hrant Dink was a member of the dwindling and often embattled Armenian minority in Turkey. He was descended from those survivors of the Genocide who had remained in the land of their birth. Hrant was born in Malatya. When he was seven years old his parents' marriage broke up and he was sent to an Armenian orphanage in Istanbul. In 1996 he established a weekly bilingual Turkish and Armenian newspaper called *Agos* ('The Furrow'). Its aim was to counteract the incessant stream of anti-Armenian propaganda in the Turkish press. Hrant Dink hoped to convey the hopes and fears of Turkish Armenians to their non-Armenian neighbours, building bridges of understanding and trust between the two communities.

Unfortunately this courageous enterprise left him open to savage attacks and deliberate misrepresentation. The journalist became a target for extreme Turkish nationalists who accused him of denigrating their country and insulting their identity. On Friday 19 January 2007 Hrant Dink was gunned down in the street outside his newspaper office. His assassin was a teenage boy from eastern Turkey whose mind seems to have been poisoned by slanted and distorted press accounts of his victim's views and beliefs. The only sign of hope from this senseless murder was the enormous crowd of people (mostly Turks) who turned out on the streets of Istanbul to express their horror and revulsion. They carried Turkish language banners proclaiming 'We are all Hrant Dink' and 'We are all Armenians'.

The back cover of *Être Arménien en Turquie*, a French translation of a collection of Hrant Dink's articles, includes a sketch by Izel Rozental. It shows the pavement where Hrant Dink was shot. Before a body is moved after a murder, an outline is drawn around it to show its original position. Instead of the outline of a man, however, Rozental has drawn the shape of a dove, with a pool of blood by its head. The artist is deliberately echoing words from the final article that the journalist wrote on the day before he was killed: 'yes, I can see in myself the anguish and anxiety of a dove, but I know that in this country people don't touch doves. Doves can live right in the heart of towns, in the hottest human crowds. Clearly not without fear – but with what liberty!'[5]

For many Armenians, both in the Diaspora and the Republic of Armenia, Hrant Dink's murder brought back bitter memories of the atrocities of the past. That a man who had dedicated his life to promoting mutual understanding between Armenians and Turks should have been eliminated in such a way was both tragic and obscene. However, the appalled reaction of many Turks to his death hints at the possibility that a time may eventually come when Armenian 'doves' and members of other vulnerable minorities in Turkey may be able to live and speak and write freely in the land in which they were born.

Colophon
Welsh doves –
St David, Morgan Llwyd and Gwenallt

Wales and Armenia are both countries with cultures shaped by centuries of Christianity. For the Welsh, as for the Armenians, doves have had a traditional symbolic significance. Noah's dove returning to the Ark on the Armenian mountain is a universal sign of the hope for a peaceful and harmonious future for humanity. The Holy Spirit is described as descending on Jesus at his baptism in the form of a dove. As a result all Christians use the dove to represent a concept that would otherwise be very difficult to portray. In Wales, the Holy Spirit as dove takes on a particular significance because of its connection with St David.

The dove makes two appearances in Rhygyfarch's life of our patron saint. The first is during his education. His hagiographer remarks that 'the holy David learned the rudiments, the psalms, the readings of the whole year, the masses, and the divine office; and there his fellow pupils saw a dove with a golden beak playing about his lips, and teaching him, and singing the hymns of God'.[6] The inference is that St David had a special relationship with God, through the Holy Spirit, from his childhood onwards.

The second intervention of a dove is better known and is the reason why pictures and statues of St David often show him with a dove perched on his shoulder. According to Rhygyfarch, 118 Welsh bishops and a vast number of other clergy and laity had gathered at a place called Brefi for a synod to discuss the Pelagian heresy, which seemed to be gaining ground. The crowd and the noise and confusion were so great that even though a pile of clothes had been heaped up to form a makeshift pulpit, hardly anyone could hear the bishop who stood on top of it. Things were getting out of hand, when someone remembered that there was a 119th bishop who hadn't turned up: David, who had been consecrated bishop by the Patriarch of Jerusalem himself (and had no doubt met several Armenians on his pilgrimage to the holy city).

Messengers were sent to fetch David. He agreed to go with them. On the way to Brefi he restored a dead boy to life. When David reached the synod, his fellow-bishops asked him to speak. He consented – but refused to stand on the (no doubt rather precarious) pulpit made of piled-up garments. Instead, he told the boy whom he had just raised from the dead to put a handkerchief on the ground. 'Standing on it, [David] explained the Gospel and the law, as if from a trumpet. Before everyone's eyes a snow-white dove, sent from heaven, settled on his shoulders and remained there as long as he preached.'[7] The scene deliberately echoes the description of Christ's baptism in the Gospels. The descent of the dove, representing the Holy Spirit, is a sign of divine approval of David's teaching, and leads the synod to choose him unanimously as Archbishop of Wales.

*   *   *

Morgan Llwyd (1619–59) was born at Cynfal in Meirionnydd. He was drawn into the early Welsh Nonconformist movement and, once the Civil War broke out, joined the Parliamentarian army. After Cromwell's victory, Llwyd became heavily involved in the intense religious excitement of the period, and was one of those officially approved to preach the Gospel in Wales. His most famous work appeared in 1653 at a time when Llwyd felt that the Second Coming was imminent. He calculated that Christ would appear and establish his Kingdom on earth in 1656. *Llyfr y Tri Aderyn* ('The Book of the Three Birds') was one of three books Llwyd produced to prepare the people of Wales for this momentous event.

There was a particular reason for choosing birds from Noah's Ark as the *tri aderyn*. Llwyd believed that the number of years between the Creation and the Flood was to be the same as the number of years between the Flood and the Parousia (Christ's return). The Flood was therefore a pivotal moment in human history. The book is a discussion between the Eagle, the Raven and the Dove. The Eagle represents Oliver Cromwell and the state authorities. The Raven stands for all those of whom Llwyd disapproved: Royalists, Anglicans and probably Presbyterians as well. The Dove is Morgan Llwyd and his fellow 'saints': members of the radical wing of the Independents, many of them influenced by the growing popularity of Quaker ideas.

The Raven is soon refuted and flies away croaking '*Crawcc! Crawcc!*' The Dove remains to answer the many questions raised by the Eagle, who clearly feels the need for spiritual advice. Perhaps the best known exchange between the two is on the subject of inner peace:

> Eagle: But how may a man find peace of mind?
> Dove: By going into the secret room, and that room is God himself within.[8]

Llwyd (in the person of the Dove) was seeking to stress the importance of a spiritual experience that came from an interior relationship with God. He was concerned with what the medieval Armenian mystic St Grigor Narekatsi describes in the headings to his prayer-poems as 'Speaking with God from the Depths of the Heart'.[9]

* * *

David Gwenallt Jones (1899–1968) is the Welsh poet with whom I have always felt most at home. He was a deeply sacramental and incarnational poet with a strong awareness of the often disastrous and destructive shortcomings of human nature.

Doves or pigeons ('*colomennod*' covers both in Welsh) make several appearances in Gwenallt's work. Writing of Wales, he speaks of 'the Holy Spirit nesting, like a dove, in your trees'.[10] In another poem, workers forced by economic pressures to leave rural Carmarthenshire for industrial Glamorgan listen carefully for the day when they can return to their roots to find rest:

> Lifting a wing and being able to go free
> like exiled doves in the evening ... [11]

Elsewhere he compares nuns to '*colomennod pell*' ('distant doves') who have lost their way, coming from their medieval convent to the harsh weather of our modern age. He looks forward to a time when the storm will be stilled and, like Noah's dove on Ararat or the doves escaping from Father Ohan's monastery, they may once again become signs of hope:

You'll rise from the forest as you did before
with ash and oak leaves in your beak,
and stand upon the roof of heaven's halls,
and the leaves rejoicing His (Christ's) heart.[12]

Gwenallt also devotes a poem to the doves that provided a hobby and an evening respite for the working men of the industrial south Wales after the day's exhausting work. He describes how the birds were sent to the distant beauty of north Wales or rural England to be released, returning to transfigure *'ein tlodi cymdogol yn y De'* ['our neighbourly poverty in the South']:

Bits of beauty amidst the industrial haze;
the shape of the Holy Spirit above the valley.

The Holy Spirit sanctifying the smoke,
and turning the worker into a living person ... [13]

Whereas in the Armenian legend of the 'Monastery of Doves' the people were saved by being changed into doves, here it is the doves, as signs of the presence and activity of the Holy Spirit, which give humanity to the workers and bless their labour. In Wales, as in Armenia, the dove is a powerful and lasting Christian symbol.

Notes

[1] See Vrej Nersessian, *Treasures from the Ark: 1700 Years of Armenian Christian Art* (London: The British Library, 2001), p. 69.

[2] *The Teaching of Saint Gregory*, translated by Robert W. Thomson, revised edition (New Rochelle, New York: St Nersess Armenian Seminary, 2001), p. 193.

[3] *Colophons of Armenian Manuscripts 1301–1480: A Source for Middle*

Eastern History, translated by Avedis K. Sanjian (Cambridge, Massachusetts: Harvard University Press, 1969), p. 108.

4 Robert Arnoux, *Arménie 1947: Les Naufragés de la Terre Promise* (Aix-en-Provence: Édisud, 2004), p. 53.

5 Hrant Dink, *Être Arménien en Turquie* (Paris: Éditions Dominique Fradet, 2007), p. 121.

6 Richard Sharpe and John Reuben Davies, 'Rhygyfarch's 'Life' of St David' in *St David of Wales: Cult, Church and Nation*, edited by J. Wyn Evans and Jonathan M. Wooding (Woodbridge: The Boydell Press, 2007), pp. 107–55 (p. 117).

7 Sharpe and Davies, 'Rhygyfarch's 'Life' of St David', p. 145.

8 *Gweithiau Morgan Llwyd o Wynedd*, edited by Thomas E. Ellis (Bangor: Jarvis & Foster, 1899), p. 232.

9 St Grigor Narekatsi, *Speaking with God from the Depths of the Heart: The Armenian Prayer Book of St Gregory of Narek*, edited by Thomas J. Samuelian, second edition (Yerevan: Vem Press, 2002).

10 'Cymru', *Cerddi Gwenallt: Y Casgliad Cyflawn*, edited by Christine James (Llandysul: Gwasg Gomer, 2001), p. 70.

11 'Sir Gaerfyrddin', *Cerddi Gwenallt*, p. 105.

12 'Y Lleianod', *Cerddi Gwenallt*, p. 106.

13 'Colomennod', *Cerddi Gwenallt*, p. 144.

5

Words

Unexpected echoes

'I love the sun-baked taste of Armenian words', wrote the poet Eghishe Charents.[1] Those words have many forms: Armenians may speak the Western or Eastern variants of their language, or chant its classical form during the Liturgy, or amusingly imitate a different dialect, as my guide and driver did on one of my visits to the country – gently mocking the distinctive way in which Iranian Armenians speak. However it soon becomes clear that Armenian, whatever the qualifying adjective attached to it, is an essential part of their identity. The Armenians, like the Welsh, believe in the old slogan once used in *Cymdeithas yr Iaith* rallies: '*heb iaith, heb galon*' ('without a language, without a heart').

Armenian and Welsh belong to different branches of the Indo-European family, although many Armenian words are derived from other ancient Near-Eastern languages. Theories about linguistic origins are subject to fiercely-fought battles and shifts of fashion and emphasis. There is, however, something particularly intriguing and attractive about the suggestion that the original heartland from which the Indo-European languages emerged was 'to the East of Asia Minor, in a rectangle formed on the three other sides by the Armenian highland plateau, northern Mesopotamia and northern Iran'.[2]

Languages transmute in all kinds of ways as they move through space and time, and apparent coincidences may sometimes be deceptive.

Nevertheless, when words from two branches of the same linguistic family resemble one another it is tempting to assume a connection originating in the distant past. Welsh-speakers are often startled to stumble across Armenian words that seem strangely familiar. Often these refer to very basic items, or objects that have been in use from a very early period. For example, '*aror*', the Armenian for 'plough', is remarkably close to '*aradr*', its Welsh equivalent.

When I first decoded the Armenian letters on a bottle of mineral water, I was astonished to discover that '*water*' is '*jur*' (pronounced 'joor'), which is extremely close to our own word '*dŵr*'. Even '*garejur*', the related word for '*beer*' (which, if Xenophon is to be believed, was almost certainly invented by the Armenians), is not too far from the Welsh '*cwrw*'. The Armenian for wine is '*gini*', which again is similar to our '*gwin*'.

A frequently repeated Armenian proverb is '*Haiastan, karastan*' ('Armenia, land of stones').[3] 'Stone' in Armenian is '*kar*', which is clearly linked to the Welsh '*carreg*'. One of the most famous prehistoric monuments in Armenia is the collection of over 200 carefully arranged stones, many of them with small holes through them. They apparently formed some kind of observatory and date back to before 2000 BC. The site is known as Karahunj, which has inevitably led to comparisons with Stonehenge. When we visited these fascinating stones, I confessed to Naira, my guide, that I was in fact an honorary druid in the Gorsedd of Bards. She got very excited about this, so I had to carefully explain that my druidic status was cultural rather than religious.

Another Armenian word appearing to have a Welsh

parallel is '*kuyr*' for 'sister', which is intriguingly similar to '*chwaer*'. My latest flash of linguistic inspiration came when I discovered that the Armenian for 'head' is '*glukh*'. This immediately made me think of the Welsh '*penglog*', meaning a skull. The head, and in particular the skull, played an extremely important role in pre-Christian Celtic religion, which may have some connection with this possibly very ancient echo. There are, however, some apparent similarities that have to be dismissed as purely fanciful. A dear Armenian friend has tried very hard to convince me that the name of the country's second city, Gyumri, is related to Cymru, our name for our homeland. I'm afraid that, to me, this seems to be no more than a happy coincidence of sound without any philological basis.

The consonant shifts between Eastern and Western Armenian, the two modern forms of the language, have a special fascination for someone who speaks Welsh. We are used to mutating the beginning of words under certain grammatically-defined circumstances. Some of the variations between the two types of Armenian resemble the Welsh soft mutation. To take examples from the names of letters of the Armenian alphabet: the second letter is '*pen*' (western) and '*ben*' (eastern), the third is '*kim*' (western) and '*gim*' (eastern) and the fourth is '*ta*' (western) and '*da*' (eastern) – which may, of course, be no more than an interesting linguistic curiosity.

The speakers of many languages have at least one word they feel to be uniquely their own and which appears to be untranslatable. In Welsh that word is *hiraeth* – a sense of longing and loss that tears at the heart-strings and can never be consoled. It was therefore quite a shock to come across an explanation of the word *garod* in a novel by the Lebanese Armenian author Kevork Ajemian. Shavarsh Sarhadian, the central figure in the book, is responding to a request by his American girlfriend to teach her his language. He remarks:

> You see, *garod* is a word unique to the Armenian language. It has no equivalent in any other. It means *longing*, missing people, places. But for Armenians it is something more than that, it is part of our very essence, a clue to our past. It is the secret driving force of our endurance ... It's all that is left of our ancient history.[4]

Even more than the linguistic echoes, the experiences that have given birth to Welsh *hiraeth* and Armenian *garod* help to create a special bond of sympathy between our two peoples.

Triad
Three masters of words

i) St Mesrop Mashtots
In the orchard next to the church are a family of thirty-six *khatchkars*. Each one of these intricately carved stones incorporates a cross and one of the original letters of the Armenian alphabet. They are the work of Ruben Nalbandyan, 'Master of the Stone-Cross Art', and mark the 1,600th anniversary of that alphabet. The church alongside them in the village of Oshakan contains the tomb of St Mesrop Mashtots, the extraordinary man who changed Armenian from an oral to a literate culture, transforming its destiny and

ensuring its survival. The author of the guide-book somewhat unkindly dismisses the building as 'most unattractively renovated' with 'unappealing frescoes'.[5] For the Armenian pilgrims who flock there, however, it is a sacred place because of the saint whose body has lain there since the fifth century. Lighting a candle at his tomb, I shared their sentiments.

Mesrop Mashtots began his career as a scribe at the court of King Vramshapuh of Armenia. Feeling a call to the monastic life, he became a *vardapet* and began preaching the Christian Gospel in one of the wildest areas of the land. In theory Armenia had been a Christian country for a hundred years, since the conversion of King Trdat by St Gregory the Illuminator. In fact, as Mesrop soon discovered, the change had often been extremely superficial. He realised that the essential problem was one of language. Because Armenian had not yet been written down, church services, including readings from the Bible, were either in Syriac in King Vramshapuh's domains, or in Greek in those parts of Armenia under Byzantine domination. Although the clergy would sometimes give an impromptu paraphrase of Scripture readings into Armenian, everything else was incomprehensible to all but a tiny minority of their congregations.

The spiritual crisis resulting from this superficial Christianity was compounded by a major political threat. The western part of Armenia had been absorbed by the Byzantine Empire. The eastern area, in the Persian sphere of influence, retained its independence under King Vramshapuh. However, the future of his dynasty was becoming increasingly precarious. It was probable that the Persians would assume direct control of the country in the near future. An Armenia split between two superpowers, with a fairly nominal religion expressed through languages that were not its own, might well lose its identity altogether. The key to its survival would be the creation of an Armenian alphabet. Spurred on by the blessing of Catholicos Sahak, a descendant of St Gregory the Illuminator, and the encouragement of King Vramshapuh, Mesrop Mashtots undertook this task.

At first it seemed straightforward. A Syrian bishop named Daniel had already been working on a prototype Armenian alphabet. But when Mesrop and his collaborators began experimenting they found that Armenian sounds and syllables were far too complex to be properly expressed by Daniel's letters. So the *vardapet* and his disciples travelled to Syria to work on an alphabet of their own. It was there that, according to Koriun, his pupil and biographer, Mashtots 'with his holy hand ... became the father of new and wonderful offspring – letters of the Armenian language, and then and there quickly designed, named, determined their order and devised the syllabication'.[6]

A rather more dramatic account of how this occurred is given by the historian Moses Khorenatsi. He describes how Mesrop Mashtots, after a long and frustrating search in which he had fruitlessly consulted a variety of scholars and experts, ended up in the town of Samosata. There he decided that the only solution was to pray about the problem. As he prayed he had an experience that, Khorenatsi says, was neither a dream nor a vision, but something that appeared 'in the depths of his heart ... to the eyes of his soul'.[7] He saw a right hand tracing the letters of the new alphabet on rock. Their shapes remained there like footprints in the snow. Mesrop memorised them and later described them to Rufinus, the Hellenistic hermit and calligrapher with whom he was staying. His host turned them into a script.

It had thirty-six letters (two more would be added in the Middle Ages to cover new words borrowed from western European languages). Both Koriun and Khorenatsi regarded the Armenian alphabet as a gift from God. The sacred nature of the letters was emphasised by their order. They began with *ayb*, the initial letter for *Astvats* (God), and ended with *ke* for *Kristos* (Christ). Mesrop Mashtots used the new script to translate the Bible, which in Armenian became known as *Astvatsashunch* ('Breath of God'). He started with the opening verse of the Book of Proverbs: 'To know wisdom and instruction, to perceive the words of understanding ...' Soon a great many important Greek and Syriac religious texts were translated into Armenian, several of which now survive only in their Armenian version.

Both Koriun and Khorenatsi tell us that Mesrop Mashtots also provided alphabets for the Caucasian Albanians (who then lived in what is now Azerbaijan) and the Georgians. Patriotic Georgians dispute this, being unwilling to admit that they are beholden to an Armenian for their script. Modern Armenians are often able to cope with a wide variety of alphabets: Armenian, Cyrillic, Roman, Greek and Arabic. Sayat Nova was an eighteenth-century Armenian troubadour whose poetic and musical career was destroyed by his infatuation with a Georgian princess. He ended his days as a monk and a martyr. His lyrics were composed in Georgian and Tatar as well as in his mother-tongue, using the appropriate script for each language. In one Armenian poem he gives himself good advice, setting out this self-instruction in triads (like the *tribannau* of Glamorgan folk poets of the same period). One remark seems especially apt:

> Three things tie the body to the soul.
> Love alphabets. Love writing. Love books.[8]

I imagine that St Mesrop Mashtots would have agreed with every word.

ii) St Grigor Narekatsi

The Vernissage is Yerevan's weekend open-air market, selling second-hand books, carpets, paintings, jewellery, miniature models of Holy Etchmiadzin Cathedral, KGB memorabilia and almost anything else that you can imagine. Browsing among its many stalls, I found one devoted to religious artefacts. They included several icons. The writing on three of them was Armenian. This surprised me. Icons have always played a fairly marginal role in Armenian Christianity. There is no iconostasis in Armenian churches. Instead there is a curtain in front of the stage on which the altar is set. It is closed during certain key moments in the *Badarak* (Liturgy), and for the entire service during Great Lent.

One of the icons in particular attracted my attention. Its subject was a saint with a furrowed forehead and prominent eyebrows, large oval eyes, slightly curly brown hair tucked behind impressive ears, a distinctly Armenian nose and a neat beard and moustache. In one hand he grasped a cross of the type held by Armenian clergy while preaching, with the other he clasped a Gospel book with a golden, bejewelled cover. His face was surrounded with a gilded halo. The saint's red and blue robes and the orange background reminded me of the tricolour flag of the Republic of Armenia.

I tried to move on from the icon, but the saint's piercing eyes kept drawing me back to it. In the end, after a bit of haggling, I offered the stallholder everything I had in my wallet (50 US dollars) for it. He agreed, slipped the icon into a fragile plastic carrier bag, and handed it over to me. Back in my hotel room I started to decode the Armenian inscription. The first part was easy: 'SB GRIGOR' obviously meant 'St Gregory'. The other word, 'TSGNAVOR', was more mysterious. After struggling with the intricacies of the Armenian alphabet, I eventually located it in the *Macmillan Armenia Armenian-English Dictionary*. 'TSGNAVOR' meant 'hermit, anchorite; recluse, ascetic' – it was a description that might well have been applied to any number of sixth-century Welsh saints. Grigor, however, was very obviously an Armenian.

But who exactly was he? The answer that immediately suggested itself was St Gregory the Illuminator (Grigor Lusavorich), the Armenian patron saint. He had spent the closing years of his life in a hermit's cave. But the Grigor in the icon was a comparatively young man. He also did not seem to be a bishop. Every portrait of St Gregory the Illuminator that I had ever seen had emphasized his episcopal status. He is always shown wearing one of those enormous and impressively decorated medieval-style mitres that Armenian bishops adopted around the time of the Crusades. This Grigor had nothing on his head.

One evening, I strayed into a bookshop on Abovian Street, and found a copy of the collection of prayer-poems of St Grigor Narekatsi, recently translated by Thomas Samuelian. Armenians either call the work *Narek*, after the monastery where its author lived and wrote, or *Matean* (which simply means 'book'), because they set it alongside the Bible as a source of spiritual influence and inspiration. Folk religion has ascribed all kinds of healing properties to the volume. Narekatsi claimed that it was intended not just for Armenians, but for the whole world. However, his astonishing verbal inventiveness and poetical skill have been a constant stumbling-block for translators. The result has been that, until very recently, the *Narek*'s influence has been confined to its author's own people and a handful of scholars from elsewhere.

St Grigor Narekatsi lived from 951–1003 in the southern Armenian kingdom of Vaspurakan. His father, Bishop Khosrov Andzevatsi, was the author of a famous commentary on the *Badarak*. Grigor spent his life as a contemplative monk in the monastery of Narek on the southern shore of Lake Van. His uncle Anania, a gifted theologian and man of prayer, was the abbot. It was a comparatively peaceful period in Armenian history, though the church was troubled by heretical movements that created suspicion and animosity in ecclesiastical circles. A fourteenth-century poem tells how three inquisitors were sent to investigate St Grigor himself. He prepared and cooked three doves, and invited the three men to eat with him. The inquisitors were horrified. It was a fast day. Only a heretic would ignore the fact. 'Eat the birds, or tell them to fly away,' Grigor said. 'But you've cooked them and put skewers through them,' the inquisitors complained. Grigor raised his hand. Feathers grew back on the birds. They hovered seven times over his head. He blessed them and they flew away. The accusation of heresy was immediately withdrawn.

We know little (apart from that delightful legend) about St Grigor Narekatsi's outer existence, but to compensate we know an extraordinary amount about his inner life. Samuelian takes as the title for his translation the words with which the mystic begins each of his prayer-poems: *Speaking with God from the Depths of the Heart.* Narekatsi journeys with searing and painful honesty into the depths of his own being, and seeks to draw his readers into the same sort of intense examination of the dark corners of their hearts. There is no place for self-delusion and the process initially is extremely uncomfortable – almost unbearable at times, particularly for those used to the cosy self-indulgence of much modern spirituality.

Perhaps it's not surprising that some modern critics have condemned St Grigor Narekatsi's work as neurotic or masochistic. That is not my personal experience. 1 have now lived with the Narek (admittedly in English and French translation) for several years, praying some of its prayers each day. Once the initial shock – achieved by a sometimes merciless heaping up of adjectives, comparisons or contrasts that would have made any medieval Welsh poet proud – is over, something else becomes apparent. Beyond the poet's merciless analysis of our human failure (which the horrors of the twentieth century confirmed yet again) there is a deep awareness of God's love and mercy shown in Jesus Christ, which becomes a profound source of hope and healing. Annie and Jean-Pierre Mahé are not exaggerating when they describe St Grigor Narekatsi as 'one of the greatest consolers of humanity', setting him alongside Buddha and Francis of Assisi.[9] As Narekatsi himself puts it, speaking with God from the depths of his heart:

> ... you visit the mercy of your light
> in the pitch blackness of the dark side of the soul,
> to cure, pardon and give us life.
> O force that cannot be deterred,
> to you glory in all things ... [10]

The author of those words turned out to be the St Grigor of my icon, which was based on a miniature from the earliest surviving manuscript of the *Narek*. Perhaps it is not surprising that his piercing eyes made such an impression on me as I wandered through the open-air market in Yerevan.

iii) **Nahapet Kuchag**

The tragic nature of so much of their history can sometimes lead to rather misleading generalisations about Armenians. Fitzroy Maclean, for example, describes them as 'dour and dogged, hard workers, hard fighters and hard bargainers'.[11] There is much truth in what he says, of course, but it also leaves a lot out. The impression he gives is that Armenians are somehow miserable and humourless. Most of the Armenians whom I have met have a huge capacity for enjoyment (often involving dancing) and an enormous sense of fun.

Tserun is one of the most delightful Armenian miniature painters. He lived in Vaspurakan in the fourteenth and fifteenth centuries and produced brightly coloured, almost cartoon-like illustrations of events from the Gospels. My favourite is one that seems to encapsulate the cheerful side of Armenian life. It depicts the moment in the wedding at Cana when Jesus has just turned the water into wine. Jesus and two disciples sit on the right hand side of the bridegroom. Our Lord has a gentle smile, and his two followers give each other knowing looks. On the left hand side a disciple is pouring some of the transformed liquid into a jug, while his companion is already drinking some of it.

The dominant figure, sitting on a throne in the middle of the picture is the bridegroom (the bride is not depicted). Where Jesus and his apostles have haloes, he has a large and impressive green and red Mongolian hat, which is presumably a sign of his social status. He is slightly cross-eyed, perhaps through having sampled a bit too much wine already – and now he has just tasted the best wine (formerly water), which to his amazement has been left till last. Somehow the miniaturist has managed to capture his slightly inebriated but extremely cheerful feeling of surprise and delight.[12] The enterprising owner of an Armenian vineyard reproduces this miniature on the labels of some of his bottles of wine.

The poetic equivalent of Tserun is a troubadour named Nahapet Kuchak. The historical Kuchak died at the end of the sixteenth century and only a small number of poems can be reliably attributed to him. However, his name has become attached to a large number of *hayrens* or stanzas, many of which were probably written a century or two before his time. They are, for the most part, concise love poems, with colourful imagery and tongue-in-cheek humour. The unhistorical Kuchak is a would-be Casanova who, like our medieval Welsh poet Dafydd ap Gwilym, may not always have been as successful in his would-be courtships as he had hoped.

Strangely enough, Nahapet Kuchak provided my first introduction to Armenian culture. As a deeply impoverished research student in Aberystwyth, with a hunger for books and an enthusiasm for poetry, I was always on the lookout for bargains. One day, in a box of items reduced for sale, I came across a volume of poems with a tattered cover. Its original price had been a princely £1.10, but it was now going for 15p. The author was Desmond O'Grady and the book contained his translations from Irish, Italian and Armenian poetry. To be honest, it was the translations from the Irish that attracted me. My maternal grandfather was a fluent Irish-speaker and I have always felt guilty about not having mastered the language.

However, when I took the volume back to the attic where I lodged, it was some lines from one of the fifteen Armenian love poems (ascribed by O'Grady to 'Mahabed Kuciag') which caught my attention:

> Whoever pays love with money
> Should burn for it. Love
> Should be paid with a red apple
> And a few grains of sugar.[13]

Translations of lyric poetry are always difficult. Decades later, on a second-hand bookstall in Yerevan, I found Ewald Osers' translations of a hundred and one of Kuchak's *hayrens*. He had put greater effort into echoing Kuchak's poetic form and rhyme-scheme and the result was rather different:

The kind of love that's bought and sold
merits burning at the stake:
True love is a sweet heavenly gift
of apples and of sugar-cake.[14]

That suggests to me that, although it is possible to get a flavour of the skill and wit of the Nahapet Kuchak poems in translation, the only way to appreciate them fully is to master sufficient Armenian to read them in the original. Perhaps that is true of poetry in any language. However, one thing that does become clear, even through the mists of translation, is that, despite the sadness of much of their history, Armenians have a delight in beauty and a wonderful capacity for enjoyment.

Colophon
Language, translators, and mystics

Those of us who live a part of our lives through a minority language are always aware of the pressures that language faces. There have to be places where nothing else but that language is spoken, and people whom you would never think of addressing in any other language. My great- grandfather spoke fluent Welsh. Somewhere between Llansilin and Croesoswallt his son, my grandfather, lost the language. Later, sadly and with cruel irony, my grandfather lost all language: a stroke deprived him of speech for the closing years of his life. My father was a prisoner-of-war in Germany and Poland from 1940 to 1945. He preserved his sanity by learning Welsh along with some of his fellow prisoners. He came to read and write the language, but was never able to speak it. I still have an orange notebook with 'Property of the Canadian Red Cross' on the cover, containing a Welsh translation of the Everyman edition of Gerallt Gymro that he made during those years. He also left me a copy of *Y Ffordd yng Nghymru* by R. T. Jenkins with the Nazi censor's stamp (*Oflag VI/B*) on the inside cover.

If my father was unable to pass the language on to me, he was at least able to awaken my interest in it. His encouragement helped me bring Welsh back into the family in my twenties. Other factors, however, were also important. When I became curate in Aberystwyth (having done a two-month *Wlpan* and immersed myself in Welsh literature) my rector put me in charge of Eglwys y Santes Fair, a Welsh-language church, and told its congregation not to speak English to me. Despite the initial oddness of my 'learner's Welsh', they were willing to do as he asked – and soon the thought of speaking *yr iaith fain* to me never crossed their minds. I have also been fortunate to serve in a series of parishes where the Welsh-speaking culture is still strong enough for me to live and minister through it much of the time.

The erosion of traditionally Welsh-speaking communities is a tragedy of which anyone who has lived in Wales over the past few decades is painfully aware. Bishop Vahan, the Armenian Primate in Great Britain and Ireland, recently told me that Western Armenian, his mother-tongue, is facing a similar crisis. It is the language of the part of the Armenian Diaspora descended from survivors of the Genocide that took place in Turkey during the First World War. Many of them settled in Lebanon, Syria, Cyprus, Jerusalem and Iraq in communities that have since been greatly eroded and dispersed as a result of conflicts in the Middle East. Those who emigrated to France and the United States (and Britain, for that matter) live in cultures where another language is overpoweringly dominant. Transmitting the mother-tongue through to the fourth or fifth generation is increasingly difficult.

Eastern Armenian, the language of the Republic of Armenia, does not have quite the same problem. Although it has been, to some extent, under pressure from Russian, it is now the language of a state with an education system and a framework of support. For Western Armenians, however, the loss of their language is a tragedy that stems from, and adds to, the suffering of the past. It is sometimes described as a 'white genocide'. That is why it is always a profound delight to hear 'sun-baked' Armenian words on any occasion.

* * *

William Morgan, the translator of the first complete Welsh Bible in 1588, is the nearest that we have to St Mesrop Mashtots. Bishop Morgan did not invent an alphabet: by his time Welsh had already been a written language for many centuries. He did, however, ensure that the project begun by his predecessors William Salesbury and Bishop Richard Davies would be brought to completion, and that the church-goers of Wales would be able both to hear Scripture and take part in the Liturgy in their mother-tongue. The twentieth-century poet David Gwenallt Jones describes how *'gras syfrdanol i'r Cymry oedd clywed Y Tad, Y Mab a'r Ysbryd yn parablu yn Gymraeg'*[15] ['It was an amazing grace for the Welsh to hear the Father, the Son and the Spirit speaking Welsh']. Armenian congregations must felt a similar astonished delight when they heard the Bible in their own language for the first time. St Mesrop Mashtots' grave has been venerated as a place of pilgrimage since the early fifth century. Bishop William Morgan is buried somewhere in St Asaph Cathedral – though no one is sure exactly where. We have never been desperately good at commemorating the true heroes of our faith and our culture in Wales. Perhaps we could learn something from the Armenians.

* * *

Coming across Thomas Samuelian's translation of the *Narek* took me back to my days as a curate in Aberystwyth when I first discovered the hymns of Pantycelyn, Ann Griffiths and the other poets of the eighteenth-century religious revival in Wales. They were concerned with *profiad* – spiritual experience. The result is that their hymns flow out to God from the heart, in exactly the same way as St Grigor Narekatsi's prayer-poems.

Shortly before my first visit to Armenia in 2005 I was invited to Llanfihangel-yng-Ngwynfa to preach and assist at the Eucharist in a service held to commemorate the bicentenary of the burial of Ann Griffiths, Dolwar Fach, in the churchyard there. Reading the *Narek*, with Mount Ararat on the horizon, a verse from the Welsh mystic inevitably came to mind:

> However strong the storms are,
> and the swell of the sea's waves,

Wisdom is the pilot,
And his name is mighty Lord.
In spite of the deluge of sin
and corruption of every kind
I shall escape in the end
Because the ark is God.[16]

Great Christian mystics like the hermit-poet from the shore of Lake Van and the hymn-writing farmer's wife from the Montgomeryshire hills are on a shared wavelength that transcends barriers of space, time and language.

Notes

[1] Eghishe Charents, *Land of Fire: Selected Poems*, translated by Diana Der Hovanessian and Marzbed Margossian (Ann Arbor, Michigan: Ardis, 1986), p. 23.

[2] Marc Nichanian, *Ages et Usages de la Langue Arménienne* (Paris: Editions Entente, 1989), p.51

[3] Dora Sakayan, *Armenian Proverbs: A Paremiological Study* (Ann Arbor, Michigan: Caravan Books, 1994), p. 99.

[4] Kevork Ajemian, *A Time for Terror* (Dulles, Virginia: Books International, Inc., 1997), p. 135.

[5] Nicholas Holding, *Armenia with Nagorno Karabagh*, second edition (Chalfont St Peter: Bradt Travel Guides, 2006), p. 113.

[6] Koriun, *The Life of Mashtots*, translated by Bedros Norehad (New York: Armenian General Benevolent Union of America, 1964), p. 31.

[7] Khorenats'i, *History*, p. 320.

[8] 'Listen to Me', Der Hovanessian and Margossian *Anthology of Armenian Poetry*, p. 111.

[9] Grégoire de Narek, *Tragédie: Matean oɫbergut'ean – Le Livre de Lamentation*, translated by Annie and Jean-Pierre Mahé (Louvain: Peeters, 2000), p. 4.

[10] Narekatsi, *Speaking with God from the Depths of the Heart*, p. 252.

[11] Quoted in *Armenia Observed*, edited by Ara Baliozian (New York: Ararat Press, 1979), p. 196.

[12] The miniature is reproduced in Hravard Hagopian, *Tzerun* (Yerevan: Mashtots Institute of Old Manuscripts – 'Matenadaran', n.d.), pl. 5.

[13] 'Yesterday I saw a young girl', Desmond O'Grady, *Off Licence* (Dublin:

The Dolmen Press, 1968), p. 35.

14 'But yesterday, on a fine day', Nahapet Kuchak, *A Hundred and One Hayrens*, translated by Ewald Osers (Yerevan: 'Sovetakan grogh' Publishing House, 1979), [p. 113], poem 43.

15 'Yr Esgob William Morgan', *Cerddi Gwenallt*, p. 229.

16 'O am gael ffydd i edrych', *Emynau a llythyrau Ann Griffiths ynghyd â'r byrgofiant iddi gan John Hughes, Pontrobert, a rhai llythyrau gan gyfeillion*, edited by E. Wyn James (Newtown: Gwasg Gregynog, 1998), p. 27.

6

Churches

A village church

The village church in Berdzor is new. Small but perfect, it is built in traditional Armenian style and stands on the site of a church that was destroyed many years before. We arrived there on the morning of Holy Cross Sunday, just in time to catch the closing stages of the *Badarak*. Berdzor is on the road that links Artsakh (Nagorno-Karabagh) to Armenia. It is a key strategic point in what used to be called the 'Lachin Corridor'. Should the long-lasting ceasefire between the Armenians of Artsakh and the government of Azerbaijan break down, it will not be long before Azeri jets swoop down along the valley to attack the settlement and its people and obliterate their church once again.

I was startled to find that I immediately felt at home at the church in Berdzor. The people who gathered in and around the building might well have come from one of the Carmarthenshire hill communities where I ministered for seventeen years. A cluster of teenage boys had gathered along the outside wall of the church. They were shyly eyeing up a group of giggling girls who stood a few yards away. There was something strangely familiar about the men, who were sitting on stones and tree trunks in front of the church entrance, smoking and exchanging the occasional word. They might almost have been from Abergorlech – and I couldn't help wondering if they were discussing the price of sheep.

Inside the priest was concluding his prayers on the

stage-like dais in front of the altar. A choir of girls (possibly more pious or musical than their counterparts outside) were chanting tunefully. A young family came in and the father helped his children to light candles. The members of the congregation were a mixture of ages. The children stood with their mothers or grandmothers. The language and liturgy were uniquely Armenian, but the atmosphere of a village church was immediately familiar. An awareness of the vulnerability of this community, which could so easily become the victim of political decisions taken in far-away meetings between powerful strangers with all kinds of vested interests, made the experience even more poignant.

Boghos Levon Zekiyan, the distinguished Armenologist, has written a brilliant article in which he discusses the three-fold understanding of the church, as expressed in the writing of the fifth-century Armenian writer Eghishe. He writes:

> Both in her active and receptive dimensions she is ... a compact community united in the solid bonds of Christ's faith and love, infused and nourished by the sacramental life. Although a social body by her very nature, the Church is also an indivisible reality in her single members. Within each Christian are expressed and realized the life of grace and God's glorification. Finally, all the spiritual reality of the Church, both in its social and personal dimensions, finds its symbolic expression, in the fuller sense of an effective and actualizing signification, in the image of the material building, a privileged place for the assembly of the faithful.[1]

In other words the Church has a social dimension as the Body of Christ in the world, a personal dimension in the spiritual pilgrimage of each individual, and a material dimension in the church building with its particular symbolism.

The social and material dimensions were still very much evident in the village church at Berdzor. The personal dimension is, by its very nature, something hidden. It is expressed through the 'speaking with God from the depths of the heart' exemplified by St Grigor Narekatsi's collection of prayer-poems. In their analysis of that work Annie and Jean-Pierre Mahé have demonstrated how the author related the individual's spiritual development to the architecture of Armenian churches in his time.

The shy boys, the giggling girls and the men having a smoke outside the church in Berdzor were following a long Armenian tradition. Byzantine critics of the Armenian Church during the Middle Ages used to take it to task for not making its people enter the church during the Liturgy. Many of the laity preferred to stay in the enclosure outside the doors while the service was going on. During the tenth century this led to the development of the *gavit* or *zamatun*: an entrance hall in front of the church. It could be used for activities that were not permitted within the church itself: the burial of the nobility and the erection of memorials in their honour and the holding of all kinds of meetings, for example. It was also a good place for those who did not actually want to go into the church, but wished to be within earshot of the *Badarak*.

This architectural innovation gave a three-fold structure to Armenian church buildings. The way in was through the *gavit*, which technically was not actually a part of the church. This led to the body of the church, where the worshippers stood. Beyond them was the sanctuary: a raised stage with the altar at its centre and steps leading up on either side. This was (and is) reserved for the clergy taking part in the Liturgy. At certain points in the service a curtain is drawn across to hide the sanctuary from the congregation. The Mahés have discerned a structure in the *Narek* that mirrors that of the church.

The reader of St Grigor Narekatsi's prayer-poems begins outside in the *gavit* or enclosure, feeling too sinful and unworthy to go any further. It is only after profound self-examination and confession, and a declaration of faith in Christ, that he or she is able to go on to the next stage, entering the body of the church beneath the dome which is a symbol of Heaven. There the penitent can join the worshippers for communal prayer and sharing in the sacraments. The final stage is, in the Mahés' words, to progress to the 'holy of holies', going 'behind the altar curtain to experience invisible realities'.[2] Thus the pattern of the church building itself provides a blueprint for the Christian's pilgrimage towards God. It is hardly surprising that churches play such a central part in traditional Armenian culture.

Triad
Three churches that have survived against the odds

i) The Katoghike (Yerevan)

Katoghike is the Armenian for 'cathedral' and is used for two buildings in Yerevan. Yet there could be no greater contrast than that between the huge new

Cathedral of St Grigor Lusavorich and the tiny medieval chapel formerly hidden away off Abovian Street that shares the same grand title. Perhaps the latter's name stems from the Armenian sense of humour – or from the affection in which the little Katoghike is clearly held, and which ensured its survival even during the worst of times. In 1936 a seventeenth-century church on the site was being destroyed as part of a Stalinist programme that combined urban development in Yerevan with the removal of religious buildings. During the process of demolition there was a surprise discovery. A small thirteenth-century church was hidden within the larger building. It was the oldest Christian structure in the capital and Armenian public opinion insisted that it should be preserved.

This was not easy at the height of Stalin's purges. The problem was solved in a splendidly Armenian way. The area in which it stood became the courtyard of the Academy of Sciences, and that building and others protected it from being seen from the main boulevard. Visiting commissars from Moscow would pass by in their limousines without realising that the little church was still there. Its survival was testimony to that combination of ingenuity, doggedness and determination that have guided the Armenians through so many crises.

When I first visited the little church it was in use as a place of private prayer and a steady stream of individuals came there for a few minutes of quiet communion with God. On my second visit a requiem service was taking place in the Katoghike and a large crowd of worshippers were gathered around the entrance. Armenians hold a requiem forty days after a funeral. It seems to me to be a very sensible idea. In my pastoral work I have noticed that the sense of loss often only fully comes home to a bereaved person some six weeks after the death of a loved one. That can be the time when the support of family and friends is invaluable.

On my last visit to Yerevan I had a surprise. The buildings around the Katoghike had been demolished, leaving the tiny building looking rather vulnerable and lonely in the middle of a patch of waste ground. A billboard revealed that there was a plan to build a much larger modern church and attach it to the medieval chapel. I felt sad. The special charm of the Katoghike had come from its small size and its being hidden away. It was the urban equivalent of those medieval Armenian monasteries built at the far end of remote valleys to keep them safe from invading Mongol hordes.

I was interested to notice that Claude Mutafian, the distinguished French Armenian historian, has also been critical of the 'regrettable solution' to the rehabilitation of the Katoghike. While obviously appreciating 'this elegant medieval chapel', he regrets the demolition of the former Academy of Sciences Building, which he sees as 'testimony to an epoch and a culture'.[3] While not being able to share in that particular kind of architectural nostalgia, I can't help but feel that bringing Yerevan's secret ecclesiastical gem out into the open has deprived it of much of its symbolic importance and its deepest significance.

ii) The Church of the Mother of God and the Seven Wounds, Gyumri

Gyumri, known as Leninakan under the Soviets,

Alexandropol under the Tsars, and Kumairi before that, is the second city in the Republic of Armenia. It was devastated by the appalling earthquake that hit the north of the country in December 1988, claiming at least 25,000 lives and leaving half a million people homeless. Twenty years later, when I visited the city, many of the scars still remained. On its outskirts are the derelict shells of blocks of half-built flats that were supposed to house the survivors. Work on these decidedly un-earthquake-proof buildings was abandoned when the Soviet Union collapsed. The mass graveyard with its rows of headstones, many of them with children's faces engraved on them, brings home the magnitude and the horror of the disaster. Sitting in a restaurant in Gyumri, I noticed that the television in the corner of the room was showing news footage of an earthquake in China. For me it was something remote and unrelated to my own experience. For some of those around me it mirrored the darkest days of their lives.

The Church of the Mother of God and the Seven Wounds was built in the nineteenth century. Its architecture reflects the Russian influence of the Tsarist period that has left its mark on many of the older buildings in the city. The church is one of two in Gyumri's main square. The other was extremely badly damaged and is still being restored. The Mother of God and the Seven Wounds also suffered in the earthquake. Services are held there regularly, but I noticed that some restoration work was still going on at the time of my visit.

We arrived there just after the morning service. My guide introduced me to the parish priest: a gentle Iranian Armenian, who looked as though he was probably in his seventies. 'He wants you to see his greatest treasure,' the guide whispered, and the old man ushered me into a side chapel parallel with the altar. A picture was propped up on a shelf that had been covered with a white cloth. Candles had been lit in front of it, and several worshippers stood to one side, deep in prayer. 'This picture was painted by Saint Luke himself,' the old priest insisted in a tone of voice that defied anyone to contradict him.

I looked at the painting closely. It depicted Christ after he had been taken down from the cross. Rays of light streamed from his seven wounds. His mother Mary looked down at his broken body in anguished love. My critical sense asserted itself. The painting was certainly not by Saint Luke, despite the priest's confident assertion. It seemed to come from a much later period. It might possibly be a painted copy of one of the Counter-Reformation prints brought to Armenia by Roman Catholic missionaries. Even so, there was something about the face of the Mother of God that reminded me of the portrayals of Mary in the earlier miniatures bound into the Etchmiadzin Gospel – pictures that have been dated to the late sixth or early seventh century.

Then the atmosphere of devotion overwhelmed me and my critical sense suddenly evaporated. It no longer mattered when and where and by whom this icon had been made. What was important was its message to the bewildered and bereaved believers of Gyumri. They knew all about broken bodies – they had scrabbled with their bare hands to try in vain to rescue their loved ones from the ruins of shoddily constructed concrete death traps. The picture of Christ's corpse reminded them of those whom they had lost. His agony was their agony. Yet the light flowing from his wounds pointed towards something else: the possibility of resurrection and even of ultimately being reunited with children, parents, husbands, wives, brothers or sisters whose shattered remains now lay in the vast cemetery.

The woman weeping over her dead son had a special meaning for the bereaved mothers of the city. Mary knew what they were going through. She shared that jagged emptiness at the centre of their existence. The sword that pierced their hearts had pierced her heart also. Their tears and her tears were mingled together. They could pour out their deepest feelings to the Mother of the crucified God knowing that she would take their hand and lead them through that desolate darkness. Having encountered such a companion and comforter, the exact provenance of an ancient picture became completely irrelevant.

After I had spent a few awestruck minutes in front of his greatest treasure, the old priest quietly led me away and said an Armenian prayer and gave me his blessing. My guide was taken aback by this. '*Kahana e!*' ('He's a married priest!'), she hissed – referring to me, and assuming that I would somehow be outraged or insulted. I wasn't. I was profoundly moved and felt extremely small and inadequate in front of this unassuming priest who had quietly shepherded his flock through a disaster of almost unimaginable horror, and had given them comfort and hope at a time when their faith and his must have been tested to the limit of its endurance.

iii) Gandzasar
The village of Vank in the heart of Nagorno-Karabagh

has a rather surreal atmosphere. It is dominated by an extraordinary hotel, built to resemble an ocean liner. The small community also boasts a swimming pool carved out of the river-bed, an internet café, a public convenience with an attendant, a zoo inhabited by some rather depressed and depressing wild animals and birds trapped in the surrounding hills, and a well-equipped school that, on my first visit there, was bedecked with balloons and flags as the children celebrated the last day of term. The walls along the side of the main road are decorated with a large number of Azeri car number-plates, discarded when Nagorno-Karabagh declared independence. I was told that Vank had benefited greatly from the largesse of one of its sons who had become a wealthy entrepreneur in Russia, but had still not forgotten the needs of his birthplace and its people.

'Vank' is Armenian for monastery, and the village gets its name from the monastic complex of Gandzasar on the hill above it. The main building is the strikingly beautiful Church of St John the Baptist, which was consecrated in 1240. At that time Gandzasar was the spiritual and cultural heart of eastern Armenia, dominated by the Hasan-Djalalian family. From the fifteenth century it became the seat of the Catholicos of the Caucasian Albanians, a title that was abolished several hundred years later. In the early eighteenth century efforts to obtain the liberation of Armenia with the help of Peter the Great of Russia were co-ordinated from Gandzasar under the leadership of Catholicos Esayi Hasan-Djalalian. A century later the monastery enjoyed a brief renaissance under Archbishop Baghdasar Hasan-Djalalian, who installed a printing press brought from Germany and re-established a theological seminary, but the monastery went into decline after his death in 1856.

Since Nagorno-Karabagh won its independence Gandzasar has recovered its significance as a spiritual centre and focus of pilgrimage. This is partly because its church is an extraordinarily attractive building, described by two architectural historians as 'tall and graceful in profile with its predominant and central dome'.[4] The rich decoration around the dome is rather unusual for an Armenian church (the other famous example being the Church of the Holy Cross on the island of Aghtamar in Lake Van). It includes reliefs showing the glorified Christ and Adam and Eve, patrons holding models of the church, and an extraordinarily serene figure of the crucified Christ, with two kings kneeling on either side of him and two bird-like angels perched on the arms of the Cross.

However, far more significant even than its aesthetic qualities is the fact that the church of Gandzasar has survived at all. It was at the centre of one of the most crucial battles of the Nagorno-Karabagh War. A hard-headed military historian describes it as 'the Monte Cassino of Nagorno-Karabagh' and adds that 'Unlike Monte Cassino, Gandzasar did not fall. Although pilgrims can dig fragments of missile casing from the monastery walls, the splendid church, described as the most culturally important building in Karabagh, was miraculously undamaged.'[5] This was extraordinary in an engagement in which the defenders, including the local priest armed with an AK47, not only fought off the Azeri army but actually brought down thirty-three planes and gunships with their anti-aircraft missiles.

The words 'miraculous' and 'miracle' recur

frequently at Gandzasar. The militant priest who had taken part in the battle told an American Armenian author that 'Despite the terrible bombardments not a single bomb exploded on the church; the bombs fell on the dome and rolled down its sides. This church is under divine protection.'[6] Even where there has been damage it is regarded as having resulted in a special blessing. The monastic outhouses were destroyed, but under their ruins were found some beautiful medieval *khatchkars* that no one had known about, and which are now proudly displayed. Visitors are also shown a missile lodged in the perimeter wall of the monastery. The fact that it did not cause any damage is also regarded as miraculous, though when I saw it I couldn't help wondering how our Health and Safety Executive would respond to the idea of an unexploded bomb being turned into a tourist attraction.

Perhaps a key to the miracle of Gandzasar may lie in the crucified Christ below the dome: a figure whose calmness and serenity has an almost Buddhist feel to it. This is a Saviour who has conquered even as he is crucified. The two kings kneeling at his feet point towards him in recognition of his power and sovereignty. But then again the miracle may have something to do with the tradition that the head of St John the Baptist, who challenged the tyrant Herod and has always been greatly revered by Armenians, is buried beneath the church at Gandzasar and gives it his protection. Others point to angels as the source of the miracle. It is said that, at the height of the battle, the shape of two angels appeared on the walls of the sanctuary of the monastery church. Hence, the strong local belief is that angels sent by God flew above the dome, deflecting the Azeri shells and missiles and keeping Gandzasar from harm. At Gandzasar you enter a world where time and eternity intersect and almost anything seems possible.

Colophon
Sacred spaces, suffering, and angels

The idea of sacred spaces – places where, in T. S. Eliot's words, 'prayer has been valid' – may seem a curious one to the doggedly secular or spiritually indifferent. For those accustomed to praying, however, sacred spaces form necessary points of reference. Whenever I need to become still and aware of God's presence, I imagine myself in such a place. It may be the sacrament chapel of the church of the Anglican monastery where I trained for the priesthood. Part of our rule of life there was to spend twenty minutes in silent contemplation each morning. I still remember the stone floor beneath my knees, the sound of the birds outside and the light filtering through the high plain-glass windows.

Or else it is the little church in Brechfa where I used to say my daily *Boreol Weddi* during the seventeen years I spent as parish priest there. Sometimes I would quietly sit cross-legged in front of the stained glass east window with its three figures: gentle-eyed forgiving Jesus, shaggy-bearded John the Baptist and St Teilo, whose face had for some reason been modelled on that of the hymn-writer William Williams, Pantycelyn. There were moments of peace and healing there, when I would be aware of the flowing waters of the Pib and Marlais streams in the background – the sound that must once have formed the background to the prayers of the medieval monks of Tallyllychau who farmed that patch of land, and even to those of St Teilo himself, back in the sixth century.

Of course, there would also be times of anger, frustration and despair. Mornings when I would stomp up and down the little church like the Psalmist on one of his off-days, telling God exactly what I thought of him. There are times when prayer is painful: confronting the suffering of much-loved parishioners and one's own anguish and doubt – or, perhaps less nobly, coping with bruised pride or the fear of having been forgotten or abandoned. But even then, in the end the stillness would win out. The stained-glass Christ in the window conveyed a message of an incarnate God who understood because he had been there himself.

I have no idea about the inner spiritual life of Armenians (apart, perhaps, from that of St Grigor Narekatsi a thousand years ago) – and I know that generalisations are almost always misleading and sometimes completely wrong. Nevertheless, having quietly watched some Armenian women at prayer in Yerevan and elsewhere, and having repeatedly stumbled across the little shrines with sacred pictures and candles that appear in so many apparently abandoned Armenian churches, it seems permissible to suggest that a great many Armenians still have a strong sense of the sacredness of certain places.

An awareness of sacred space was once a very strong part of Welsh spiritual life. It is something that can often be rekindled by visiting ancient centres of pilgrimage like St David's Cathedral, or St Govan's Chapel wedged halfway down its Pembrokeshire cliffside, or the remote valley of Pennant Melangell. Yet it is also important that we, like our Celtic forebears and like many devout Armenians, discover our own particular patches of holy ground: places where we can come close to God and God can come close to us.

* * *

Armenians know more than any other Christian people about the experience of suffering and the difficulty of reconciling that experience with the concept of a loving God. The American-Armenian theologian Vigen Guroian describes an episode from the Genocide:

> One day in 1915, as in so many Armenian towns and villages, the 800 families of Kourd Belen ... were given orders to evacuate their homes and form a caravan of deportation. The pastor of the village was an eighty-five year old priest, Fr. Khoren Hampartsoomian, who for all his years as a priest had served the people of Kourd Belen. Fr. Hampartsoomian was instructed to lead his people out of the village. As the procession of bewildered, frightened, and disoriented Armenians left the outskirts of the village, nearby Turks came out to view the exiles, and taunted the priest, calling to him, 'Good luck old man. Who are you going to bury today?' The old man replied: 'Yes. God is dead, we are rushing to his funeral.'[7]

Guroian suggests that the old priest may have felt like the crucified Jesus, who also asked why God had forsaken him, and comments: 'perhaps at that moment Khoren Hampartsoomian experienced the near destruction of the soul – that ultimate desolation – which became also the experience of the Armenian people.'[8]

A writer who experienced that same desolation was

Vahan Tekeyan, one of the few major Western Armenian poets to survive the Genocide. Tekeyan was in Cairo when war broke out in 1914, and so escaped the Turkish round-up of Constantinople's Armenian intellectuals in the following year. By 1917 Tekeyan had been following the savage annihilation of Turkey's Armenians with a growing horror that led him to question his faith. If the Armenians were indeed to be totally wiped out, he wrote:

> let us swear that when we find
> God in his paradise offering comfort
> to make amends for our pain,
> let us swear that we will refuse
> saying No, send us to hell again.
> We choose hell. You made us know it well.
> Keep your paradise for the Turk.[9]

Yet only seven years later Tekeyan would write a paean of praise to the Armenian Church, seeing it as having played an essential part in his people's survival:

> Against storms, our church is haven and harbour.
> Against the cold night, it is fire and flame.
> It is the shaded forest in the heat of day
> Where lilies flower, watered by our hymns, our
> psalms.
>
> The Armenian church knows the secret road to
> heaven
> hidden under every stone. For the Armenian spirit
> and body it is the shining armour, its crosses
> swords;
> its bells reverberate with the victory we know is

ours.[10]

Perhaps that 'secret road to heaven' may be enshrined in the form of the Trisagion (the 'thrice holy' prayer) that the Armenian Church uses 'for the days of the Cross, of the Church, of Saints and of Fasting':

> Holy God, holy and mighty, holy and immortal,
> Who wast crucified for us,
> Have mercy upon us.[11]

It's a prayer that has led to a great deal of theological debate over the centuries. The Armenian Church has been accused of saying that God the Holy Trinity suffered on the Cross. It categorically rejects this distortion, pointing out that it believes that only the Second Person of the Trinity (God in Christ) was crucified. This means that through Christ, human suffering is brought into the Godhead, and God knows and understands the reality of that suffering.

One of the greatest twentieth-century figures of the Church in Wales came to the same conclusion. Timothy Rees was a Cardiganshire man who became an Anglican monk and was eventually consecrated Bishop of Llandaff. He served as a chaplain in the trenches during the First World War and was awarded the Military Cross for his courage there. In the Flanders mud he came face to face with appalling suffering and the death of many of those whom he was caring for, often in horrific circumstances. Somehow he had to reconcile this misery with his belief in a loving God. He could only do so through contemplating Christ on the Cross. His theology of suffering is most clearly summed up in two of his hymns. In one he speaks of the way in which:

> ... when human hearts are breaking
> Under sorrow's iron rod,
> The same sorrow, the same aching,
> Wrings with pain the heart of God.

In the other he sees that the anguish of a suffering world is in itself a continuation of the agony of the 'Crucified Redeemer':

> The groaning of creation
> Wrung out by pain and care;
> The moaning of a million hearts
> That break in dumb despair.
> O Crucified Redeemer,
> These are Thy cries of pain!
> O may they thrill our selfish hearts
> Till love come in to reign.[12]

Amidst the pain and misery of the Western Front the Welsh chaplain became aware of a mystery that the Armenian Church had contemplated for centuries: the crucifixion of God in Christ for our sake.

*   *   *

Armenians never seem to have much difficulty in believing in angels. Welsh Christians are often more sceptical (though someone once told me that a survey had shown that 60 per cent of British people believe in them). I celebrate the Eucharist 'with angels and archangels and all the company of heaven' several times a week, and so I tend to take their existence for granted. When I spent a memorable week on Iona, I often got the feeling that, if I turned around quickly enough, I might glimpse one of St Columba's angels. In the monastery of Tatev in the mountains of southern Armenia the sense of a protective angelic presence was very strong. One Christmas, as I skidded blindly down the mountain in a blizzard after the Midnight Mass in Llanfihangel Rhos-y-Corn, I was certain that only Michael and his angels could get my little Fiat home safely. They did.

The angels that protected the ancient monastery during the battle of Gandzasar may remind some people of the 'Angels of Mons' during the First World War. The latter had their origin in a short story by the Anglo-Welsh writer Arthur Machen, which first appeared in the *Evening News*. It caught the public imagination at a time of great anxiety, and soon everyone knew someone who knew someone else who had seen the 'angels'. Gandzasar is different. As Patrick Wilson Gore remarks, 'the monastery and its ancient church ... have an air of holiness apparent to even the least religious of visitors'.[13] It would be very difficult not to believe that angels somehow played a part in its miraculous survival.

Notes

[1] Boghos Levon Zekiyan, 'Ełišē as witness of the ecclesiology of the early Armenian Church' in *East of Byzantium: Syria and Armenia in the Formative Period*, edited by Nina G. Garsoïan, Thomas F. Mathews and Robert W. Thomson (Washington, District of Columbia: Dumbarton Oaks Centre for Byzantine Studies, 1982), pp.187–97 (p. 195).

[2] Grégoire de Narek, *Tragédie*, p. 174.

[3] *Les douze capitales d'Arménie*, edited by Patrick Donabédian and Claude Mutafian (Paris: Somogy, 2010), p. 232.

[4] Bagrat Ulubabian and Murad Hasratian, *Gandzasar* (Milan: OEMME

Edizioni, 1987), p. 10

5 Patrick Wilson Gore, *'Tis Some Poor Fellow's Skull: Post-Soviet Warfare in the Southern Caucasus* (New York: iUniverse, Inc., 2008), pp. 91-2.

6 Vahé Oshagan and Ara Oshagan, *Father Land* (New York: powerHouse Books, 2010), p. 15.

7 Vigen Guroian, *Faith, Church, Mission: Essays for Renewal in the Armenian Church* (New York: The Armenian Prelacy, 1995), p. 92.

8 Guroian, *Faith, Church, Mission*, p. 92.

9 'We shall say to God', *Sacred Wrath: The Selected Poems of Vahan Tekeyan*, translated by Diana Der Hovanessian and Marzbed Margossian (New York: Ashod Press, 1982), p. 10.

10 'The Armenian Church', Tekeyan, *Sacred Wrath*, p. 33.

11 Nersoyan, *Divine Liturgy of the Armenian Apostolic Orthodox Church*, p. 49.

12 Quoted in D. Densil Morgan, *Cedyrn Canrif: Crefydd a Chymdeithas yng Nghymru'r Ugeinfed Ganrif* (Cardiff: University of Wales Press, 2001), p. 51.

13 Wilson Gore, *'Tis Some Poor Fellow's Skull*, p. 91.

7

Struggles

Blood and tears

The monastery of Makaravank is set on a mountainside in the north-eastern Armenian province of Tavush, overlooking the border with Azerbaijan. The rough track leading up to it would have wrought havoc with our usual driver's BMW, so instead we arranged for a local man to take us there in his taxi. It was a sturdy little Lada that was clearly its young owner's pride and joy. He had stuck VA-VA-VOOM in Armenian letters across the windscreen to demonstrate both his own prowess and that of his vehicle. He skilfully manoeuvred the taxi along the winding, rutted road that led towards the monastery, obviously trying to impress the sophisticated young woman from Yerevan who was acting as my guide and translator.

As we climbed up towards Makaravank we could see the sunlight reflected from the roofs of a distant village and the surface of a reservoir. 'Those are in Azerbaijan,' my companion observed. I remembered that the guide-book had warned travellers not to venture too near the Azeri border, as there was a danger of being fired on by snipers. Our driver told us that he had just returned from completing his military service in Nagorno-Karabagh, the Armenian-populated enclave that won its independence from Azerbaijan after a bitter war in the 1990s.

The monastic complex was built between the tenth and the thirteenth centuries. Surrounded by trees, it has a peaceful atmosphere. Its fame derives from the unique and fascinating carvings on the step of the *bema* (the platform on which the altar stands) in the thirteenth-century church. They include peacocks, sirens, doves, fishes, the prophet Jonah, sphinxes, a man named Yeritasard (who may have been the architect or the sculptor) and a wonderful variety of complex patterns. The dome of the older church is now incomplete, presumably as a result of the wear and tear of time, though my guide had a far more interesting explanation.

She claimed that the monastery had been built by an architect named Makar, from whom it derived its name. It was at the time that Timur the Lame and his merciless hordes were sweeping into Armenia. The local prince had conscripted all the young men of the area, including Makar's only son, in an attempt to repel the invader. The master builder was at work on the dome of the church when a messenger galloped up the mountainside towards him. 'Do you have any news of my son?' Makar called out. 'He has been killed in battle,' the horseman replied. The boy's father was so shaken by this that he blacked out, lost his footing and fell to his death. The dome was left unfinished and the monastery was named after its tragic architect.

The story is no more than a legend, yet it reflects the agonizing history of the borderland. Outside Makar's church, beneath the trees, is a recently carved *khatchkar*. It has been placed there as a monument to those who had died along the border during the fighting with Azerbaijan. They had been local farmers, fighting to protect their land from Azeri invaders, just as Makar's son had striven to keep back the hosts of Timur the Lame. When we came out of the church we found our young driver standing quietly in front of this memorial. His tears flowed as he remembered family and friends who had been killed in the conflict. There were droplets carved on the *khatchkar*. They represented both tears and drops of blood.

The following year I was in the Nagorno-Karabagh capital of Stepanakert, which is roughly the same size as Carmarthen. We visited a museum dedicated to the 'perished *azatamartiks*' – the freedom fighters who lost their lives during the Karabagh Armenians' struggle for independence in the 1990s. Its walls are lined with the photographs of those who died. They are country people, many of them young men who look as though they would have been quite at home in the Dyffryn Cothi Young Farmers' Club. Their faces are a far more telling testament to the cost of war than any list of names or compilation of statistics.

The exhibits include examples of the home-made firearms and other weaponry produced by the Karabaghtsis during their desperate fight for survival. There are some sketches drawn by one of the militiamen during a lull in the fighting, not long before his death. They include Christ in glory, Christ on the Cross, an old-fashioned sailing ship, and a picture of a beautiful bare-breasted young woman (either the artist's girlfriend or some imagined ideal). The musical instruments that the soldiers used to entertain themselves include a broken guitar. Its owner smashed it when he heard that his best friend had been killed in battle.

In a glass case are a pretty white wedding dress, a smart black suit and the linked crowns worn by the bride and bridegroom during an Armenian marriage ceremony. They were given by Galya Aroustamyan, the courageous and remarkable woman who founded the museum. The wedding dress belonged to Galya's daughter. The suit should have been worn by the girl's fiancé. Before their marriage could take place he died in the fighting. The photographs of the two young lovers whose future together was so suddenly destroyed are a reminder of the way that war tears people's lives apart, shattering their hopes and dreams and possibilities.

Galya Aroustamyan declares that 'the border of the Armenian land passes through our hearts'. She writes of the memorial that she has created: 'Each visitor to the museum takes away with him a sincere relic and leaves a small part of his own heart. And [the] soul of the perished soldier inspires: "May we be the last victims of war," it whispers, predicting peace and rest, "the last war ..."'[1] It is a powerful hope and prayer that has been uttered after many conflicts – and yet, despite the long-lasting ceasefire, the future of Armenian Artsakh (Nagorno-Karabagh) remains uncertain. Azerbaijan has oil. Armenia has none.

Triad
Three battles for Armenian freedom

i) Avarayr

In 1984, in a fit of curiosity, I sent off for a newly-published edition of Archbishop Tiran Nersoyan's translation of the *Divine Liturgy of the Armenian Apostolic Orthodox Church*. Browsing through the attractively-bound volume I came across something that puzzled me. Among the familiar feasts and categories of holy men and women included under 'the variables for principal holy days' was one group that I had never heard of. The section was entitled 'For the Vardanians', and opened with the words:

A victor filled with supernal power,
Valiant among soldiers, O blessed Vardan.
Holy martyr, chosen Vardan, ordained captain of
the host.
Many fellow-soldiers with thee were proved holy
and brave martyrs.
Imbrued in their rose-coloured blood, they
inherited the kingdom.
They saw the heavenly light and were deemed
worthy of the crown.[2]

I am ashamed to admit that twenty years would pass
before I discovered who the heroic Vardan and his
brave Vardanians actually were.

Vardan Mamikonian came from an Armenian noble
family that was said to be of Chinese origin. He
inherited the hereditary post of *sparapet* (commander-
in-chief) of the Armenian army at a time of crisis. The
ruling dynasty had died out in 428, leaving Armenia
without a king. From then on the country was ruled by
a governor appointed by the ruler of Persia. In 439
Yazdagerd II ascended to the Persian Throne. Both he
and his chief minister, Mihr-Narseh, were fervent
Zoroastrians. Armenia had been Christian since St
Gregory the Enlightener's conversion of King Trdat in
301. A century later the introduction of the Armenian
alphabet and the translation of the Bible and the
Liturgy had greatly strengthened the country's
religious identity.

The Armenian political and clerical leaders held a
council in which they asserted their loyalty both to the
Christian faith and to their Persian overlord.
Yazdagerd regarded this dual allegiance as both

contradictory and unacceptable. He was determined to bring Armenia into the Zoroastrian fold, even if he had to use force to do so. He summoned the Armenian nobles to his court and made them accept Zoroastrianism against their will. They did so outwardly, but would later claim that they inwardly still continued to affirm their Christian faith (like making a promise while keeping your fingers crossed behind your back as a sign that you don't really mean it).

This apparent apostasy left the Armenian nobles feeling embarrassed and humiliated. They returned home accompanied by a triumphant group of Yazdagerd's Zoroastrian missionaries. The Armenian people and clergy remained defiant. In 450 they rebelled in defence of their land and faith and persuaded the nobles to support them. The latter, having been absolved of their involuntary lapse at the Persian court, joined together in a solemn covenant and attacked the Persians. Vardan Mamikonian led them to an initial victory. However, his position began to be undermined by an ambitious noble named Vasak Siuni. The account of the war by the contemporary writer Eghishe portrays Vasak as a traitor and a coward: someone to be vilified and scorned in the same way that Americans would later despise and denigrate Benedict Arnold.

In 451 Armenia was invaded by a massive Persian army, including a large contingent of terrifying battle elephants. On 2 June it clashed with Vardan's forces on the field of Avarayr. Before the battle Vardan and the holy priest St Ghevond addressed the Armenian troops. Vardan emphasized the way in which the Persian ruler had misunderstood the depth of their

Christian commitment:

> He who supposed that we put on Christianity
> like a garment, now realizes that as he cannot
> change the colour of his skin, so he will perhaps
> never be able to accomplish his designs. For the
> foundations of our Christianity are set on the
> unshakable rock, not on earth but above in
> heaven where no rains fall, no winds blow, and
> no floods rise. Although in the body we are on
> earth, yet by faith we are established in heaven
> where no one can reach the building of Christ
> not made by human hands.[3]

Vardan's image of the indelible nature of Armenian
Christianity, as much a part of his people as the colour
of their skin, is one that Armenian religious leaders
have repeatedly returned to across the centuries.

Vardan's warriors were massively outnumbered on
the battlefield. Their position became even more
desperate when the treacherous Vasak Siuni and his
men abandoned them at a crucial moment.
Nevertheless, the Armenian commander-in-chief and
his followers inflicted massive losses on the Persians
before being overwhelmed by them. Vardan was
among the 1,036 Armenian Christians who lost their
lives in the battle. The death toll among Persian
Zoroastrians and Vasak's Armenian apostates was
3,544. Eghishe regarded the battle as a draw in which
heroes had been killed on both sides. Avarayr did not
put an immediate end to the sufferings of the
Armenians. It did, however, start the process which,
after thirty years of guerrilla warfare, would lead to the
Armenians being granted freedom of religion by their

Persian overlords. Vahan Mamikonian, Vardan's nephew, played a major role in securing this historic edict of religious toleration.

Vardan and his companions became regarded as saints and martyrs who had given their lives both for their faith and their people. This idea was significantly influenced by Eghishe's *History of Vardan and the Armenian War*, one of the masterpieces of the fifth-century 'Golden Age' of Armenian literature. Professor Robert Thomson, Eghishe's English translator, has shown how strongly the Armenian's account was influenced by the story of the Jewish Maccabean revolt against the tyrant Antiochus Epiphanes. This had been included in the translation of the Bible into Armenian less than a half a century before. According to Eghishe, Vardan and his companions modelled themselves on the Jewish heroes who had been willing to sacrifice themselves to preserve their religion and their cultural identity. Through their martyrdom on the field of battle the Vardanians won their place in the Armenian Divine Liturgy, and the battle of Avarayr became a natural reference point to which Armenians have returned throughout their history.

ii) Sardarabad

May 1918 was one of the darkest times in Armenian history. The Genocide that began in 1915 had wiped out over a million Turkish Armenians. Russian troops had abandoned Transcaucasia in the wake of the Bolshevik revolution. A Turkish army now threatened to obliterate the small area of Russian Armenia that remained in Armenian hands. That army was soon within 20 miles of Yerevan. Disaster and annihilation seemed imminent. General Silikian, the Armenian commander, visited Catholicos Kevork V, known as 'the Catholicos of tears' because of the tragic times in which he was the spiritual shepherd of his people. The soldier advised the church leader to abandon his Cathedral of Holy Etchmiadzin and seek refuge in the area around Lake Sevan. He received an uncompromising reply from the elderly Catholicos: 'If the Armenian forces cannot defend this holy place I shall do it on my own, even if I have to perish on the threshold of this thousand-year-old cathedral.'[4]

Catholicos Kevork did not have to suffer such a grim fate. On 21 May General Silikian's troops were attacked by two Turkish regiments near Sardarabad, within striking distance of Holy Etchmiadzin. The Armenians counter-attacked two days later, and in five days of fighting succeeded in driving the Turkish forces back for 30 miles. Later one Armenian officer recalled the way in which he addressed his men before the battle:

> I told them that they must realize that we could not retreat anymore because the small free territory in our rear was all that remained of Armenia and that to run for refuge in the mountains would mean to abandon not only the inhabitants of the territory but also the countless refugees who found safety there.[5]

By the evening of 23 May the Turks were in retreat. Another Armenian officer wrote: 'The battle was won. Armenia was saved'.[6]

Sardarabad took its place alongside Avarayr in the Armenian imagination. It is seen as a victory in which a cross-section of the whole Armenian nation took part. Richard Hovannisian describes how 'the Armenian soldiers ... were assisted by hundreds of civilians. Carts drawn by oxen, water buffalo, and cows jammed the roads bringing food, provisions, ammunition, and volunteers ...'[7] Next to the massive monument to the battle, erected in 1968, is the Ethnographical Museum – the Armenian equivalent of the Welsh Folk Museum (now the National History Museum) at St Fagan's, near Cardiff. At the foot of a staircase are positioned sculpted figures, representing the wide range of people of all ages and both sexes who contributed towards the Armenian triumph. They include a statue of Archbishop Karekin Hovsepiants, wearing his clerical robes and Ararat-shaped hood. In his hand is a book he uses to inspire the others. A non-Armenian visitor would probably assume that it is the Bible. In fact it is Eghishe's *History of Vardan and the Armenian War*, telling the heroic story of the battle of Avarayr.

Archbishop Hovsepiants (a distinguished scholar who later became Catholicos of the Great House of Cilicia) and Bishop Zaven Papazian rode to the front on horseback to encourage the troops, following the example of the patriotic priest St Ghevond in 451. The link between the battles of Avarayr and Sardarabad is emphasised by many Armenian writers. Bishop Grigoris Balakian describes the 1918 battle as 'this epic victory of the second Avarayr'.[8] Serge Afanasyan calls it 'a source of inexhaustible inspiration', adding that 'it proves that, fifteen centuries after Avarayr, the blood of the heroes who achieved the greatest moments of its history still flows in the veins of this martyred and dispossessed people.'[9]

After the Bolshevik revolution Armenia, along with

Georgia and Azerbaijan, formed the Democratic Federative Republic of Transcaucasia. While the battle of Sardarabad was still in progress this fractious federation fell apart. Georgia sided with the Germans and Azerbaijan formed an alliance with the Turks. The fledgling independent Republic of Armenia had to seek support from allies in Western Europe who were not desperately reliable or committed. The battle of Sardarabad did not put an end to the many threats and dangers that the Armenians faced. It did, however, show that they had the capacity both to win an unexpected victory and to survive when all the odds seemed stacked against them.

iii) Shushi

Visitors to the hillside town of Shushi in Nagorno-Karabagh (or Artsakh as it is known to Armenians) are taken to see a tank, painted in green with white crosses to signify the army that it belonged to. The tank is a reminder of a battle whose origins lay in a disastrous decision taken by a British general many decades before. In November 1918 General W. M. Thomson arrived at Baku in Azerbaijan to take over command of the Allied forces in eastern Transcaucasia. His approach to the problems and conflicts of the area were governed by two primary considerations. Firstly, he was interested in the fate of the oilfields around Baku, and he particularly wished to prevent them from falling into the hands of the Bolsheviks. Secondly, he wished to gain the support of the Muslim population of Azerbaijan. Any action that might alienate Muslim opinion within the British Empire – and particularly in the Indian Raj – was to be scrupulously avoided.

This had grim implications for the Armenian

Christian population of Karabagh. General Andranik, a guerrilla fighter of almost legendary status, was asked by Karabagh's Armenian leaders to provide them with military assistance. He was on his way to the Karabagh capital of Shushi when he met a delegation sent by General Thomson. The latter told the Armenian general that, since the Great War was now over, the borders of Armenia would be settled by the peace conference at Versailles. If he brought his army into Karabagh he might prejudice a decision that would favour his people. Andranik accepted the word of the British general and withdrew his forces. Then in January 1919 Thomson appointed a notorious anti-Armenian as provisional governor of Karabagh.

This politician, Dr Khosrov Bek Sultanov, shared the views and philosophy of the Turkish leaders who had been responsible for the Genocide. The tensions and sporadic massacres that resulted from his leadership culminated in the destruction of the Armenian section of Shushi and the death of many of its inhabitants. Ironically, they had represented the most moderate group among the Karabagh Armenians, desperately attempting to reach some sort of compromise with Sultanov and his henchmen. The dead included a churchman who was the leading advocate of this conciliatory approach. Bishop Vahan Ter-Grigorian had his tongue torn out. He was then decapitated and his head was put on a spike and paraded triumphantly through the streets.

General Thomson's catastrophic approach to Nagorno-Karabagh would be compounded by Stalin. After the incorporation of Armenia and Azerbaijan into the Soviet Union, the Communist Party's Caucasus Bureau, under Stalin's watchful eye, decided in July

1921 that Nagorno-Karabagh should become an autonomous region within Azerbaijan. This was part of Stalin's divide-and-rule policy for dealing with nationalities in the Soviet Union, though it may also reflect the anti-Armenian prejudice he sometimes showed as a Georgian. The relationship between the predominantly Armenian enclave and the government of Azerbaijan became increasingly difficult as the decades went by. The Armenians of Nagorno-Karabagh felt discriminated against and under threat. In February 1988, encouraged by Gorbachev's talk of reform, the local soviet asked Moscow to allow the region to join Armenia. The request was turned down.

The situation deteriorated. Armenians were massacred in the Azerbaijan industrial town of Sumgait. In September the Armenian inhabitants of Shushi were forced to leave their homes. By January 1990 guerrilla warfare had broken out in Nagorno-Karabagh. Initially Azerbaijan received the backing of Soviet forces. In September 1991 both Armenia and Nagorno-Karabagh became independent republics. As the conflict intensified, the strategic importance of Shushi became clear. The city, with its walled fortress, stands on a hill above the Nagorno-Karabagh capital of Stepanakert. The latter was systematically bombarded from Shushi by batteries of Grad missiles and other armaments.

To add insult to injury the Azeris stored their missiles in Shushi cathedral, which had been taken over for secular use in Soviet times. They felt that the Armenian Karabaghtsis were unlikely to attack such a sacred building. The bombardment was constant. One of those who very nearly fell victim to it was Bishop Parkev Martirossian, who had been busy reestablishing Christianity among the Armenians of Artsakh. He was awakened one morning by the characteristic noise of Grad missiles being fired, and immediately got up to pray for his people in Stepanakert. Shortly afterwards a missile landed on the bed where he had been sleeping.

On 8 May 1992 the Karabaghtsi Armenians launched a frontal attack on Shushi. Their soldiers had exactly the same uniforms as the Azeris, so they painted white crosses on their field jackets and equipment. They may have remembered the heroes of Sassoun in the Armenian national epic, who always went into a fight with the mark of the battle-cross on their shoulders. Twelve hundred Karabaghtsis were facing 3,500 Azeris. Nevertheless, only sixty Karabagh Armenians lost their lives in the battle, against about 200 Azeris and mercenaries. Two of the Karabagh casualties were crew members of tank number 442 – the T-72 with its white crosses, which was the only tank that the Karabaghtsis possessed. It was knocked out by an Azeri tank, but not before it had escorted the Karabagh infantry up the hill towards victory. It is preserved as a memorial to the battle and those who died in it. Before mid-day on 9 May Shushi was in Karabaghtsi Armenian hands

Beneath the enormous statue of Mother Armenia that looks down on Yerevan (replacing an equally massive statue of Stalin that was pulled down with great delight when the dead dictator fell from official favour) is a museum of the Nagorno-Karabagh War. Like the NKR Museum of Perished Azatamartiks in Stepanakert, it has a gallery of photographs of those who lost their lives. Placed at their centre, however, is a reproduction of one of the most powerful images of modern Armenian iconography. Khandjian's giant tapestry of the *Vardanank* – the warriors of Avarayr – was made in 1983 and is kept at Holy Etchmiadzin. The detail from the tapestry that is set among the faces of the dead freedom-fighters is that of St Vardan himself. He is a powerful bearded figure with an intense expression, mounted on a white horse. His right hand grasps his unsheathed sword and his left hand signals his fellow warriors to continue their resistance. An angelic figure places a wreath above his head: a halo that is a sign of the martyr's victory. The museum's displays include a model of the battle of Shushi. As at Sardarabad, there are echoes of Avarayr, the unforgettable Armenian heroic sacrifice.

Colophon
Arthur, Catraeth, memorials

When St Vardan and his warriors faced their Persian enemies in the middle of the fifth century, our own people were going through an equally testing crisis. The Roman legions had left. The Romano-British or Brythonic kingdoms that remained were under attack from almost every direction: Saxons and related tribes from the east, Irish from the west and Picts from the north. As in Armenia a Christian hero did emerge: Arthur is the nearest that we can get to Vardan. Unfortunately there was no Eghishe to write his story. Brythonic was going through the linguistic nervous breakdown from which it would emerge as Welsh. St Patrick, writing his autobiographical letters in Latin in the early fifth century, was a Romano-British Christian, probably from Wales. (The distinguished Early and Medieval Welsh scholar Sir Ifor Williams made a case for the apostle of Ireland having been the first-recorded Welsh speaker.) But Patrick pre-dated Arthur and so does not refer to him.

Some people doubt that Arthur ever really existed. Thomas Charles-Edwards is prepared to concede that 'there may well have been an historical Arthur', but adds that 'the historian can as yet say nothing of value about him ...'[10] Two fairly early references to him, however, give us a tantalising glimpse of a Christian hero in the same mould as St Vardan. The ninth-century Welsh historian Nennius describes how Arthur won twelve victories against the Anglo-Saxon invaders. He remarks that 'the eighth battle was in Guinnion fort, and in it Arthur carried the image of the holy Mary, the everlasting Virgin, on his [shield], and the heathen were put to flight on that day, and there was a great slaughter upon them, through the power of Our Lord Jesus Christ and the Holy Virgin Mary, his mother.'[11] An anonymous tenth-century Welsh annalist adds a detail (which has a distinctly Armenian feel to it) about another of Arthur's triumphs: 'The Battle of Badon, in which Arthur carried the Cross of Our Lord Jesus Christ for three days and three nights on his shoulders [i.e. shield] and the Britons were the victors.'[12]

The figure of Arthur would evolve over the centuries in the pseudo-historical fantasy of the twelfth-century writer Geoffrey of Monmouth and a variety of folk stories and romances. Geoffrey's imaginings about Arthur left their mark on Welsh historians for many centuries. However, as Theophilus Evans, one of the greatest Welsh prose writers of the eighteenth century, remarked, 'it is as genuinely certain that there was such a king as Arthur, as that Alexander existed, although the life-history of them both has been clouded by old legends'.[13] One of the most distinguished contemporary Welsh historians, John Davies, thinks it reasonable to accept Arthur's existence and suggests that he won a notable victory around 496, and then was killed or disappeared after the disastrous battle of Camlan (about 515). The latter would be remembered by medieval Welsh storytellers as one of the 'Three Futile Battles of the Island of Britain' where the British/Welsh fought among themselves instead of confronting the common enemy.[14]

Echoes of Arthur still had a certain potency among twentieth-century Welsh nationalists. Saunders Lewis, the founder of Plaid Cymru, was arrested in 1936 for his part in setting fire to an RAF Bombing Training School on the Llŷn peninsula. In 1938, after his release from prison, he published a collection of political articles entitled *Canlyn Arthur* ('Following Arthur'). Gwynfor Evans, who became the first Plaid Cymru Member of Parliament, also stressed the significance of the fifth-century hero, describing him as 'a Briton from the west who spoke the language of the Welsh'. Evans remarks that 'of all the great men who safeguarded and enriched our tradition, he is the most colourful and the most mysterious'.[15] St Vardan's British/Welsh contemporary may not have had an Eghishe to record his heroism, but he continues to inspire and fascinate.

* * *

Perhaps the most bizarre attempt to establish a direct link between Wales and Armenia appeared in 1855 in a book by an eccentric scholar named G. D. Barber. The

author had got hold of John Williams ab Ithel's
translation of the *Gododdin*, an epic poem in Welsh
that most scholars now accept was composed by the
poet Aneirin around the year 600. It tells the story of a
heroic war-band gathered together by Mynyddog
Mwynfawr, the ruler of a kingdom centred on what is
now Edinburgh (a reminder that in the sixth and seventh
centuries the Lowlands of Scotland were Welsh-
speaking). The 300 warriors rode south to attempt to
drive the Anglo-Saxon invaders from the area that is
now Northumbria. Their expedition culminated in a
battle at Catraeth (the modern Catterick in
Yorkshire), where Mynyddog's army was slaughtered,
leaving only the poet and possibly three other
survivors to tell the story of the brave men who died.

Barber translated ab Ithel's translation of the
Gododdin into Aramaic. Then, having changed all the
vowels, he translated it back into English again. The
result that emerged from this improbable process was
quite extraordinary. Barber informed his readers that
the poem:

> gives scenes of Aram, Ararat or Armenia. HUD,
> the patriarch of the Arabs, and the Abram of the
> Hebrews, is the hero and primitive leader of the
> 'Cimri,' or KEN-*marah* (Great Ken), at their
> original site near Lake Van and in the subjacent
> plains of the Zab and neighbouring Ur and Uz.

He came to the startling conclusion that 'The 'Gododin'
– 'Battle of Catraeth' now appears to have for its
subject the GAME of CHESS, of which it gives general
descriptions in successive stanzas, assigning it to a
Hindu inventor, Caw, of Gomer, as in Ferdushi.'[16] This is

all utter nonsense, of course – though one cannot help feeling a slight pang of sympathy for someone who devoted so much misplaced learning and daft ingenuity to convert a battle that took place in Yorkshire at the end of the sixth century into a prehistoric game of chess on the shore of an Armenian lake.

Arthur, in the glimpses that we have of him from Nennius and the anonymous author of the early Welsh annals, is very much a Christian hero, carrying the image of the Virgin Mary or the Cross as he goes into battle. One of the *Gododdin* heroes, although undoubtedly a valiant fighter, is compared unfavourably to Arthur in the poem. The hand-picked horsemen from the Welsh-speaking lands who rode south to meet the Anglo-Saxon enemy are not usually regarded as having been motivated by the depth of faith that inspired Arthur or St Vardan. Mynyddog Mwynfawr had provided them with a great feast and copious quantities of drink before they set out. They gave their lives so valiantly, Aneirin tells us, in exchange for the mead and wine that they had received – and if 299 of them were killed, their opponents lost seven times as many.

Nevertheless, the horsemen of Mynyddog's army were Christians consciously confronting pagan invaders. Before setting out the warriors had made their confession in church. Among them was the ferocious but loveable Ceredig, whom Aneirin commends both to a place in the heavenly choir and to the presence of God the Holy Trinity:

> On his last day may he, who was a friend of song,
> know a dwelling place in the land of heaven.
> May he be welcomed among the communion of
> saints

in full union with the Trinity.[17]

Another hero of the *Gododdin* was the grey-haired but powerfully voiced Beli, whose battle-cry reflected his religious background: 'May the One who calls to heaven defend us!'[18] Ceredig, Beli and their companions might well have felt at home among Arthur or St Vardan's warriors.

* * *

Carmarthen is filled with a variety of memorials to past wars and heroes. Opposite my vicarage is an unattractive obelisk in memory of General Picton, who fell at Waterloo. A statue of General Nott, who led a nineteenth-century British incursion into Afghanistan, stands in the centre of town. A monument to the Royal Welsh Fusiliers who died in the Crimean War is in the middle of Lammas Street. Outside the Guildhall there is a memorial to the local men who lost their lives in the Boer War, while the cenotaph to those who died in the two World Wars and the Korean War was erected in Priory Street. The names of battles and of some of those who were killed in them go back for over 200 years.

Seeing the rows of photographs in the memorial museums to the Nagorno-Karabagh War in Stepanakert and Yerevan, I couldn't help wondering if pictures of the fallen would be an even more effective memorial than lists of names. Faces remind us that each one was a person made in the image and likeness of God, and therefore of infinite value. My father took part in the Second World War, my mother's father took part in both World Wars and his grandfather fought in the Crimea. Unlike them, I have never had to go to war. But the faces of two people who were killed in more recent conflicts come to mind. Pete, an American exchange student who shared a room with me during my last year at school, was killed in Vietnam. Sam, who went to the same village primary school as my sons, died in Afghanistan. Thinking of them, it strikes me that the best memorial of all would be that – as Galya Aroustamyan imagined her dead Karabaghtsi freedom-fighters saying – 'to the last victims of war'.

Notes

1   Galya Aroustamyan, *The NKR Museum of Perished Azatamartiks Guidebook* (Stepanakert: Amaras, 2009), p. 4.
2   Nersoyan, *Divine Liturgy of the Armenian Apostolic Orthodox Church*, pp. 178–9.
3   Ełishē, *History of Vardan and the Armenian War*, translated by Robert W. Thomson (Cambridge, Massachusetts: Harvard University Press, 1982), pp. 154–5.
4   Serge Afanasyan, *La victoire de Sardarabad: Arménie (mai 1918)* (Paris: L'Harmattan, 1985), p. 45.
5   Quoted in Jacques Kayaloff, *The Battle of Sardarabad* (The Hague: Mouton, 1973), pp. 34–5.
6   Quoted in Kayaloff, *Battle of Sardarabad*, p. 39.
7   Richard G. Hovannisian, *Armenia on the Road to Independence 1918* (Berkeley and Los Angeles: University of California Press, 1969), p. 193.
8   Grigoris Balakian, *Armenian Golgotha: A Memoir of the Armenian Genocide, 1915–1918*, translated by Peter Balakian with Aris Sevag (New York: Alfred A. Knopf, 2009), p. 376.
9   Afanasyan, *La victoire de Sardarabad*, p. 85.
10 Thomas Charles-Edwards, 'The Arthur of history' in *The Arthur of the Welsh: The Arthurian Legend in Medieval Welsh Literature*, edited by Rachel, Bromwich, A. O. H. Jarman and Brynley F. Roberts (Cardiff: University of Wales Press, 1991), pp. 15–32 (p.29).
11 Nennius, *British History and The Welsh Annals*, edited and translated by John Morris (London: Phillimore, 1980), p. 35.
12 Nennius, *British History and The Welsh Annals*, p. 45.

13 [Theophilus Evans], *Drych y Prif Oesoedd (Second or 1740 Edition)*, edited by Samuel J. Evans (Bangor: Jarvis & Foster, 1902), p. 130.

14 John Davies, *Hanes Cymru* (London: Allen Lane The Penguin Press, 1990), p. 57; *Trioedd Ynys Prydein: The Triads of the Island of Britain*, edited by Rachel Bromwich, third edition (Cardiff: University of Wales Press, 2006), p. 217.

15 Gwynfor Evans, *Aros Mae* (Swansea: Gwasg John Penry, 1971), pp. 55–6.

16 G. D. Barber, *Ancient Oral Records of the Cimri, or Britons, in Asia and Europe, recovered through a literal Aramitic translation of the old Welsh Bardic Records* (London: J. R. Smith, 1855), pp. vi, xiii.

17 Ifor Williams, *Canu Aneirin gyda Rhagymadrodd a Nodiadau* (Cardiff: Gwasg Prifysgol Cymru, 1970), pp. 13–14.

18 Williams, *Canu Aneirin*, p. 18.

8

Genocide

The Castle of Swallows

There is one place that every visitor to Yerevan feels compelled to visit. Foreign dignitaries often plant a memorial tree on a special plot nearby. Other people walk across the concrete and down the steps to leave a flower and say a prayer, or stand in silence in front of the eternal flame. As an *odar* (a non-Armenian), I find the sense of loss and emptiness there, and the heart-rending awareness of our human capacity for inhumanity overwhelming. I cannot begin to plumb the depths of feeling that an Armenian must experience. This is Tsitsernakaberd ('the Castle of Swallows'): the memorial to the victims of the Genocide in Ottoman Turkey during the First World War, which cost the lives of over a million Armenians.

During and immediately after the First World War the appalling atrocity was acknowledged. Some trials were even held of the main figures responsible. Several had escaped abroad and were condemned to death in their absence. Some were later assassinated by young Armenians determined that the perpetrators of such horrors should not escape without punishment. But then the political climate changed. Allied plans to carve up Turkey collapsed. The Greek invasion of Asia Minor was defeated by Kemal Atatürk's Turkish nationalist army. Both the Western powers and Soviet Russia began to woo the new Turkey. The suffering of the Armenians and the many promises made to them during and in the immediate aftermath of the Great

War were swiftly forgotten.

The word 'genocide' would not be coined until after the Second World War. In the meantime the events that would later be recognised by many as the first genocide of the twentieth century would be swept under the carpet for several decades. Those who survived often had to concentrate on rebuilding their shattered lives. The Armenian writer Kostan Zarian wrote in the 1930s:

> As for our dead, our victims and martyrs: Let them forgive us and wait. This is no time for erecting monuments. We, the living, need the stone and the mortar. We Armenians are not a nation of orphans and beggars, but builders and fighters.[1]

Nevertheless, trying to bury such an event in the back of the mind is always dangerous. A genocide unacknowledged or forgotten gives the green light for genocides to come. As was mentioned in the prologue, Adolf Hitler notoriously remarked in August 1939, 'Who remembers now the extermination of the Armenians?' Hitler would send the body of Talaat Pasha, the architect of the Armenian Genocide, back to Turkey, where his remains received a state funeral and he was interred as a national hero.

By 1965, fifty years after the beginning of the mass extermination of Turkey's Armenians, the need to acknowledge and remember had become urgent. Those who had survived the Genocide and could witness to what had happened were gradually beginning to die out. The Turkish government stubbornly refused to admit that it had ever happened.

The Soviet government had formerly taken a similar line, but now decided that a limited recognition of the horrors of 1915 might be a way of putting pressure on a country (Turkey) that had joined NATO in 1952 and was now firmly in the pro-American camp. A limited official commemoration of the fiftieth anniversary was sanctioned in Yerevan. What then happened took the Soviet authorities completely by surprise.

On 25 April 1965, while the authorised event with its carefully selected audience was taking place in the Yerevan Opera House, a crowd of about 100,000 people gathered outside. They angrily demanded that Armenian lands in Turkey should be restored to Armenia. Stones were thrown, and it took all the skill of the much-respected Catholicos Vazgen I to calm things down. The shock waves were considerable. The leader of the Armenian Communist party was dismissed and his replacement inaugurated the Genocide Monument at Tsitsernakaberd in 1967. From then onwards it became the focus of a mass national act of remembrance of the Genocide.

The Genocide Monument has two elements. One is the circle of twelve enormous basalt slabs inclined, as though in mourning, towards the central space that contains the eternal flame. That is the place of quiet reflection, with a constant background sound of ancient Armenian liturgical chants creating the sense of a sacred space. Beside the circle is a narrow, divided stele shooting up towards the sky. This symbolises the survival and renaissance of Armenia and the Diaspora and their unity. Taline Ter Minassian suggests that the rather abstract design of the monument was deliberately intended to allow visitors to interpret it in different ways. She notes, for example, that Diaspora

Armenians tend to think that the twelve basalt slabs 'represent the twelve provinces of martyred Armenia – while there are only six *vilayets* of eastern Anatolia'.[2]

What really matters, however, is not the detailed symbolism of the monument, but the concrete way in which it commemorates an event the authorities had previously deliberately ignored. Garo Kehayan describes the observance of 24 April, Genocide Memorial Day, in the newly independent Armenia of the early 1990s:

> Like the myriad cells in a single body, the entire population comes together as one on this day. Silent and sombre, over a million souls in Yerevan, not so much physical bodies as a unified field of emotion in hypnotic shuffle, wend their way to the concrete needle and massive lotus-like structure that encloses the eternal flame of the Genocide memorial, to lay a circular wall of flowers. There is no crime today, no laws are broken. Nothing unites Armenia more than this wound that is not allowed to heal.[3]

Triad
Three witnesses to genocide

i) Komitas

Many of those who took part in the street demonstration in Yerevan on 25 April 1965 carried portraits of one of Armenia's cultural heroes, who had come to symbolize the suffering of the Genocide. Komitas, whose original name was Soghomon Soghomonian, was born in Turkey in 1869.

His mother died when he was six months old. Eleven years later his father followed her to the grave. The orphan was left destitute. However, his beautiful singing voice and obvious musical talent meant that he was chosen by the local bishop to go to Holy Etchmiadzin, where he was enrolled in the Kevorkian Seminary. In 1895 he was ordained as a *vardapet*.

His interest in Armenian folk music, as well as liturgical music, led to hostility from some of the more conservative members of the Etchmiadzin community. Encouraged by Catholicos Khrimian, the young monk travelled to Berlin in 1896 to further his musical studies, and spent three years at the university there. On his return to Armenia he continued to collect folk songs, as well as conducting choral concerts. By 1906, however, he was once again feeling stifled in Holy Etchmiadzin and returned to Western Europe. There he established choirs and gave lectures, introducing Armenian music to a new audience, before returning to Armenia the following year.

The musician's life in Holy Etchmiadzin continued to be difficult. Komitas experienced both opposition and neglect. In 1909 he wrote in desperation to the new Catholicos: 'During these past twenty years I have seen only traps and injustice. My nerves are exhausted; I cannot endure any longer.'[4] He requested to be transferred to the island monastery of Sevan, where he might be able to live as a hermit and carry on his studies in peace. His plea was ignored. Komitas was rescued, however, when he was invited in 1910 to become the choirmaster of an Armenian church in Constantinople. He remained a controversial figure even there, coming under attack from some quarters for arranging concerts in secular venues with programmes that combined selections of Armenian religious chant and folk songs.

In 1911, after a visit to Egypt to arrange an Armenian choir tour, Komitas travelled to Paris to visit his long-standing friend Margaret Babaian. They went over to Shanklin on the Isle of Wight for a peaceful fortnight's holiday. Margaret later recalled:

> As we listened long to the sounds of the waves, at times so tender and at others so violent, Komitas would liken them to the sounds of the Armenian language. Sitting on the sand, he would sing new songs, while a cold British moon overhead would look down in bewilderment, unable to understand which land such ardent melodies could come from. And I was his sole audience, along with the frowning silhouette of the rocks and the rippling waves.[5]

Komitas then returned to Constantinople, though he gave some lectures in Europe the following year. Back in the Ottoman capital, he composed a song to celebrate the 1,500th anniversary of the Armenian alphabet in 1913. After the outbreak of the First World War he continued to immerse himself in his musical work. Then, on the evening of 24 April 1915, the blow fell. Without warning the intellectual, political and cultural leaders of the Armenian community in Constantinople were arrested without charge. Komitas was one of them. His servant told a neighbour that 'They took the reverend father ... The police took him during the night.'[6]

The prisoners were taken by train to Ankara and then by cart to Chankiri in the Anatolian hinterland.

Komitas seems to have been quite calm at the beginning of the journey, even comforting and encouraging his fellow prisoners. However, when the musician was about to take a drink from a bucket of fresh water, it was wrenched away by a bullying Turkish gendarme. Aram Andonian, a journalist who was to be one of the few survivors among the deportees, noted that 'Komitas was seriously frightened. He retreated back and wrapped his right arm around his head to protect it from further attacks. His face was splashed with water and it was dripping down his beard.'[7] From then onwards Komitas' condition deteriorated. Father Grigoris Balakian, a fellow *vardapet* who later managed to escape from captivity, described how:

> Father Komitas, who was in our carriage, seemed mentally unstable. He thought the trees were bandits on the attack and continually hid his head under the hem of my overcoat like a frightened partridge. He begged me to say a blessing for him in the hope that it would calm him.[8]

The prisoners reached Chankiri. Father Balakian managed to acquire an Armenian prayer book and persuaded the Turkish commander to let them hold a service of vespers. It took place 'at dusk, by dim candlelight, behind the high walls of the huge armoury of Chankiri, with the icy spring gale blowing through the open windows'. Balakian noticed how political, religious and class divisions all became irrelevant. Komitas sang the '*Der Voghormya*' ('Lord Have Mercy'), one of the most emotive and powerful of all Armenian prayers, and the gathered prisoners wept.

His fellow priest remarks:

> Perhaps Archimandrite Komitas had never in his
> life sung 'Lord Have Mercy' with such emotion.
> Normally he would sing it ex officio, as solace for
> the pain, grief, and mourning of others; this time
> he sang out of his own grief and emotional
> turmoil, asking the eternal God for comfort and
> solace. God, however, remained silent.[9]

Only forty of the 291 Armenian prisoners sent to
Chankiri survived. Komitas was one of them. It is
thought that influential admirers of his music
intervened on his behalf. The American Ambassador to
Turkey may have been one of them.

Komitas returned to Constantinople. His mental
health had been shattered by his experiences. He
became increasingly paranoid. Rita Kuyumjian, his
Canadian Armenian biographer, is also an Assistant
Professor of Psychiatry. She suggests that he was
suffering from Post-Traumatic Stress Disorder. His
illness meant that he was no longer able to continue
his musical work or function as a priest. Meanwhile the
horror of the Genocide continued remorselessly. The
Armenian villages where he had collected folk songs
were systematically wiped out. The ordinary people of
the countryside who had shown him hospitality and
sung for him were slaughtered. The Armenians who
remained in Constantinople were in an increasingly
precarious position.

Komitas' friends became more and more worried
about his mental state. In October 1916 they tricked
him into being committed to a Turkish military
psychiatric hospital. As Marc Nichanian puts it,

Komitas 'was turned over, bound hand and foot, to people who were simultaneously murdering his compatriots by the hundreds of thousands throughout the empire'.[10] It is not surprising that Komitas' illness showed no sign of improvement. Rita Kuyumjian notes that 'for Komitas, being institutionalized in a hospital run by the Turkish military was effectively no different from being held in a Turkish prison, in both situations he was in the hands of "the enemy".'[11] In 1919 he was transferred to a private psychiatric institution in Paris, and three years later, when the cost of keeping him there proved too great, to a public mental hospital. He remained there until his death in 1935. Towards the end there were signs of healing. A few months before he died he told his visitors 'to take care of the children of the Armenian nation ... to love each other, to love a lot so you can live ...'[12]

Although Komitas survived the Genocide, his brush with its horror shattered the mind of this gentle, vulnerable, sensitive and brilliant man. His remains were returned to Armenia in 1936 and his final resting place became a focus for those who wished to remember the Genocide during the years before it was officially commemorated. One of the last great poems by Eghishe Charents, who would perish as one of Stalin's victims in 1937, was his 'Requiem Aeternam' to Komitas. It describes the trauma and torment that makes the tragic musician, 'tormented like Lear', a lasting witness to the agony that overwhelmed his people:

> Like the warm fields
> of your distant country

that were parched
by a black hand,
your ringing soul
became a dry field
with neither lifegiving sun
nor thin ray of hope.

Maddened by terror,
pulled apart by nightmares, unshod,
you wore death's shroud.
And although fed by the spirit only
your soul was not wrung dry.
The blood of the martyrs
was the final
unbearable blow.[13]

ii) The skull from Deir Zor

There are three dangers in discussing the Armenian Genocide. The first is compassion fatigue. The catalogue of atrocities that were committed is so extensive and appalling that they can prove too much for us to take in. We read of the disarmed Armenian soldiers in labour battalions being forced to dig the trenches that then became their graves. We hear of the inhabitants of the Armenian quarters of towns and the population of whole villages being forced to leave their homes and sent on death marches into the desert. The men were taken aside and killed. The women were raped repeatedly, or sold off to Turks or Kurds or Arabs to be forcibly converted and turned into brides or concubines. Many of the children were auctioned as well. Some were given away by mothers who didn't want to see them starve to death. Other desperate mothers jumped over precipices or drowned themselves in the Euphrates, clutching their babies. Hunger and disease claimed many lives. We are told of priests who were tortured to death, and how, at Trebizond on the Black Sea coast, barges were filled with Armenians and then sunk, drowning their human cargoes. So much death, vouched for by reliable witnesses, despite the official attempt to hide it all. So much cruelty and pain can be difficult to take in, especially for those of us who are not Armenians. It's easier to turn away.

The second danger stems from the passage of time. The Armenian daughter-in-law of one of my acquaintances went into a shop in England and found herself being served by a Turkish woman. 'Where do you come from?' she asked. The shop-worker replied with the name of a town whose Armenian population had been wiped out in the Genocide. The daughter-in-law spat an insult at her and stormed out of the shop. 'I simply don't understand it,' my friend remarked. 'It's all happened so many years ago. Can't they just forgive and forget?' We shall soon be marking the centenary of the Armenian Genocide. It was a long time ago. Yet while the atrocity remains unrecognised and even vigorously denied the wound is still unhealed.

The third danger stems from statistics. So often the question of the Genocide is reduced to a numbers game. On the one hand dubious attempts are made to minimise the number of Armenians living in Ottoman Turkey before the First World War. The aim is to try to show that there were hardly any Armenians to obliterate, so that if they were wiped out it was only a minor massacre. This contemptible bit of sleight of hand soon comes up against concrete historical realities. The vacuum left by so many dead becomes impossible to explain away. But on the other hand more reliable statistics can often leave us numb. Huge numbers of lives were destroyed: hundreds of thousands, a million and half perhaps. The individual pain of each one can easily get lost in the massive total, which is why a single skull can suddenly acquire such importance.

I saw it on my first visit to the Genocide Museum in Yerevan. It hasn't been there on my later visits, so perhaps it was on loan, or was felt to be an unsuitable exhibit. Yet to me it brought home the meaning of the Genocide in a uniquely powerful way. It came from Deir Zor, the place in the Syrian desert that has the same resonance for Armenians that Auschwitz has for Jews. The Lebanese Armenian photographer Bardig Kouyoumdjian writes of a recent visit there: 'In the subconscious of the Armenian that I am, this name, Deir Zor, is the symbol of genocide, a mark left on the surface of the planet, the cemetery of a people.' He describes how, in front of the altar in the memorial church there, 'at the foot of the column of the resurrection, bones carpet the soil, evidence of the martyrdom of the Armenians.'[14] A photograph of these bones includes a skull like the one I saw in the museum in Yerevan.

The skull was a reminder that behind the statistics of genocide are a myriad of individuals: somebody's father or mother or sister or brother or child. Each one of them was an infinitely valuable life, swept away by a tsunami of hatred and horror. Vahan Totovents had been a student in America at the time when the Genocide began. He returned to Armenia to join his people's struggle against the Turks. In his autobiographical *Life on the Old Roman Road* (translated into

English as *Scenes from an Armenian Childhood*) he depicts his birthplace: a Western Armenian village wiped out during the Genocide. Veronica was one of the million and a half victims – not a number but a person:

> Veronica was an ethereal being, as feathery as a fawn; she had pale-chestnut eyes and the complexion of a rose ...

> The turquoise of the sky crumbled on to Veronica's head ... The deadly, parching winds blew from the desert and covered her body under the sands ... Only the morning star shed a few tears upon her, after which, evening fell with blood-stained eyes ... [15]

Totovents also describes the fate of his cousin Rebecca. She was one of those young Armenian women who were abducted and forced to forsake their religion and marry Turks, Kurds or Arabs. The Turkish human-rights lawyer Fethiye Çetin, whose grandmother was among them, says that their neighbours referred to them as 'the leftovers of the sword'.[16] Totovents' writes of Rebecca:

> She was a big, healthy, lively, intelligent, and poetic girl. Her enormous blue eyes alone would have been enough to rebuild the whole of the devastated heaven. That heaven crashed down on to Rebecca's tall white lilies. They took her to the Arabian deserts ... I heard with horrified anguish that they branded her sunny forehead and cheeks ... I bow before your terrible fate,

sister mine ... Accept a tear from a brother ... [17]

In one of his short stories the same Armenian writer tells of a young man returning to his native village after the armistice, only to discover that his entire family have been wiped out in the Genocide. His desolation echoes Totovents' own experience and that of other survivors who discovered the horrifying reality encapsulated in the phrase 'Armenia without Armenians':

> Grief, like a dense fog, descends from the sky and
>   rises from the earth.
> The golden ashes of twilight sift down on to our
>   heads, as tangible grief.
> The sun, like a stabbed heart, drains its last drops
>   of blood and departs to
> another, a happier universe ...
> It is night ... a gigantic coffin, deep and silent ...
> The lid of that dark coffin is blue and nailed
>   down with starry nails.
> The symphony of death is roaming about.
> Who is it singing that silent and pitiless
>   melody ...?[18]

iii) **The Homilies of Mush**

'Armenia without Armenians' was not only the elimination of a people. It was also the obliteration of a culture. Monasteries and churches were destroyed, converted to secular use or turned into mosques. The names of towns and villages were altered and the word 'Armenia' itself was outlawed from Turkish maps. The medieval manuscripts that are a central part of the Armenian artistic and religious heritage were obvious targets. Many of them were lost forever. Those that survived often did so because of the heroic self-sacrifice of courageous individuals. One such manuscript, which has acquired almost legendary status, is the *Homilies of Mush*. Now kept safely in the Matenadaran in Yerevan, apart from a few stray leaves that ended up in the Mekhitarist monastery of San Lazzaro in Venice, it weighs 32 kilograms (excluding the binding) and is described by Abgarian as 'the largest parchment manuscript in Armenian'.[19]

The *Homilies*, with their beautifully illuminated frontispiece and first page, were commissioned by an Armenian dignitary named Astuadsatur of Babert at the beginning of the thirteenth century. Almost as soon as the work was completed, he was killed by the local emir, who purloined all his possessions except the manuscript of the *Homilies*. It was taken by the town's judge, who claimed that the dead man had owed him money. A couple of years later the judge decided to sell it. The Bishop of Mush (to the west of Lake Van) and his clergy decided to buy it, but on their first attempt the asking price was too high. They went home and collected more money from the Armenians of their area, and finally succeeded in rescuing the volume from its captivity. It was taken back to the Monastery of the Holy Apostles (Surb Arakelots Vank) at Mush, where it was carefully preserved and treasured until the Genocide of 1915.

The Armenians of Mush suffered terribly during the Genocide. They made a desperate attempt to resist, but were overwhelmed by the Turks. The survivors were brutally massacred. A senior Turkish officer later described how more than 500 women and children were herded into a stable and burnt alive. The

Monastery of the Holy Apostles was left in ruins. Two of its treasures survived. One was a twelfth-century carved door, which has been described as 'the most spectacular work of medieval Armenian sculpture southwest of Lake Van'.[20] This was carefully smuggled by local Armenians to Yerevan, where it is now in the Historical Museum. The *Homilies* was also rescued, and an oft-repeated story is told to explain its survival.

It is said that two courageous women from Mush decided that they could not allow the monastery's most precious manuscript to fall into the hands of the Turks, who would almost certainly destroy it. So they divided it in two, wrapped it around their bodies, and set off to take it to safety beyond the Russian lines. One of the women, starving and desperately ill, managed to take her half of the manuscript to Holy Etchmiadzin, from whence it was later transferred to the Matenadaran. The other half disappeared and was presumed lost. It later transpired that the woman who was carrying it realised that she was dying and so buried it in the grounds of the Armenian Church at Erzerum. A Polish officer unearthed the manuscript there, apparently quite by chance. He took it to Baku, where he sold it to an Armenian charitable organisation. It was brought to Yerevan, where it was reunited with its partner.

The hard-headed French Armenian scholar Claude Mutafian describes this amazing narrative as 'an extremely tenacious legend ... apparently lacking any foundation'.[21] He also points out that the manuscript had actually been divided in two as far back as 1828 for purely practical reasons. Nevertheless, the way in which this treasure survived the Genocide and was brought to safety deserves some kind of legend. It is a symbol of the way in which so many Armenians, although facing almost certain extermination, were determined that their cultural and spiritual inheritance would survive.

A further example of this spirit is illustrated by another manuscript that was rescued from the destruction of the Genocide. A monastery near Kaiseri had been destroyed by the Turks. Its manuscripts were consigned to the flames. An Armenian scholar, Thadeus Jamgotchian, noticed an undamaged volume among the ashes. It was a sixteenth-century manuscript of the poetry of the medieval Catholicos St Nerses Shnorhali. Jamgotchian risked his life to rescue the book and gave it to Jane Wingate, an American missionary, asking her to keep it safe. Shortly afterwards Thadeus Jamgotchian and his family died when their house was set on fire by Turkish nationalists. Mrs Wingate took the manuscript back to America and produced the first English translation of St Nerses' best-known poem from it. She dedicated the work 'to the memory of those saintly Armenians whose Christian fortitude in the face of persecution, exile and martyrdom has been an inspiration ...'[22]

Colophon
Recognition, denial, and commemoration

There are many things that make a person proud to be Welsh. Somewhere on my list is the fact that our National Assembly in Cardiff has recognised the Armenian Genocide. We are also the first nation in these islands to have a public memorial to the victims of the Genocide. Why is this significant? The twentieth century taught us how easy it is for people to rewrite history, airbrushing out those items which they found inconvenient. In Wales we have had our own experience of this. The old encyclopaedia instruction 'For Wales see England' was symptomatic of the way in which Welsh history and culture were so often sidelined or ignored altogether.

When the subject that is eliminated from history books or dismissed from public discussion and acknowledgment is genocide, the danger is obvious. If a particular act of genocide can be dismissed as never having happened, it may encourage the perpetrators of future genocides to think that their crimes will be set aside in the same way. Yet the Armenian Genocide is still often denied altogether, or mentioned in inverted commas (to give the impression that it is somehow questionable) or qualified by adjectives like 'alleged' or 'disputed'. This is not just dangerous, it is also dishonest. As the respected historian Donald Bloxham writes at the beginning of one of his books on the subject:

> Deniers and obfuscators should not be allowed to set the agenda, and bad-faith disputes do nothing at all to promote the scholarly examination of complicated phenomena. The orchestrated murder of the Armenians is taken as a given, a starting point for discussion, not its endpoint.[23]

The Armenian Genocide happened. Even if the British Government is still too obsessed by fear of upsetting Turkey to recognise this truth, we in Wales have not shied away from it.

In 2007 I received an unexpected phone call from

north Wales. The voice at the other end of the line turned out to be that of Eilian Williams: a man of utter integrity and amazing energy, who combines farming sheep with campaigning for human rights. He had been the driving force behind the recognition of the Armenian Genocide by the Welsh Assembly. After reading an article about Wales and Armenia that I had written for *Cambria* magazine, he had decided to invite me to give one of the addresses at the unveiling of the Armenian Genocide Memorial in Cardiff. I agreed. On the appointed day I caught a train to the capital and headed for the Temple of Peace where the ceremony was due to take place.

As I got nearer the building I began to feel a bit nervous. There was clearly a large and noisy demonstration in progress. I had gathered from the *Western Mail* that some extreme Turkish nationalist groups had threatened to disrupt the unveiling, having failed in their attempts to bully the courageous director of the Temple of Peace into abandoning it altogether. A smiling man with a friendly face and a splendid moustache suddenly appeared. He must have been told to keep an eye out for a stranger wearing a dog collar. 'Don't worry,' he said as he shook me by the hand. 'I am Armenian. I come from Baghdad. I will get you in safely.' And he did.

The memorial was beautifully designed, combining elements of an Armenian *khatchkar* and a Celtic cross. It was dedicated with prayers in Armenian and Welsh. A requiem for the souls of the victims of the Genocide was chanted by Bishop Nathan, Senior Deacon Stepan and the choir of the Armenian Church of St Sarkis, who had come from London. In the background the Turkish genocide-deniers attempted to drown the beautiful singing by monotonously (and shamelessly) shouting 'Shame on you!' Two contrasting figures in the gathering around the memorial seemed to sum up the occasion, to my mind. One was a middle-aged Turkish woman who had somehow slipped through the police cordon and stood defiantly among the worshippers with a look of bullying contempt on her face. The other was a dignified elderly Armenian woman who wept heartfelt tears as she recalled family members murdered during the Genocide.

The following year, on the eve of Holocaust Memorial Day, the Cardiff *khatchkar* was smashed by a person or persons unknown. The sledgehammer used for this despicable act of vandalism was left nearby. Undaunted, the Cardiff Armenians restored the monument. It remains a focus for pilgrimage and prayer, not only for visiting Armenians, but also for their Welsh friends who are determined not to forget the victims of the systematic attempt to exterminate a people that took place in Ottoman Turkey during the First World War. While protesting against an earlier atrocity, the massacres of Armenians by the 'Red Sultan' Abdul Hamid in 1896, William Ewart Gladstone declared that 'To serve Armenia is to serve civilization.'[24]

Notes

1   Gostan Zarian, *Bancoop & the Bones of the Mammoth*, selected and translated by Ara Baliozian (New York: Ashod Press, 1982), p. 8.

2   Taline Ter Minassian, *Erevan, la construction d'une capitale à l'époque soviétique* (Rennes: Presses Universitaires de Rennes, 2007), p. 185.

3   Garo Keheyan and J. C. Tordai, *Yearning for the Sea: Armenia in the 1990s* (Nicosia: Pharos Publishers, 1990), p. 39.

4   Quoted in Rita Soulahian Kuyumjian, *Archeology of Madness: Komitas, Portrait of an Armenian Icon* (Princeton, New Jersey: Gomidas

Institute, 2001), p. 67.

5   Quoted in Kuyumjian, *Archeology of Madness*, p. 94.

6   Aram Andonian, *Exile, Trauma and Death: On the road to Chankiri with Komitas Vartabed*, translated and edited by Rita Soulahian Kuyumjian (London, Gomidas Institute and Tekeyan Cultural Association, 2010), p. 11.

7   Andonian, *Exile, Trauma and Death*, p. 129.

8   Grigoris Balakian, *Armenian Golgotha: A Memoir of the Armenian Genocide, 1915-1918*, translated by Peter Balakian with Aris Sevag (New York: Alfed P. Knopf, 2009), p. 66.

9   Balakian, *Armenian Golgotha*, p. 73.

10 Marc Nichanian, *Writers of Disaster: Armenian Literature in the Twentieth Century: Volume One – The National Revolution* (Princeton, New Jersey: Gomidas Institute, 2002), p. 41.

11 Kuyumjian, *Archeology of Madness*, p. 157.

12 Quoted in Kuyumjian, *Archeology of Madness*, p. 194.

13 'Requiem Aeternam' , Eghishe Charents, *Land of Fire: Selected Poems*, edited and translated by Diana Der Hovanessian and Marzbed Margossian (Ann Arbor, Michigan: Ardis, 1986), p. 225.

14 Bardig Kouyoumdjian and Christine Siméone, *Deir-es-Zor: Sur les traces du genocide arménien de 1915* (Arles: Actes Sud, 2005), pp. 35, 38.

15 Vahan Totovents, *Scenes from an Armenian Childhood*, translated by Mischa Kudian (London: Mashtots Press, 1980), pp. 135-6.

16 Fethiye Çetin, *My Grandmother: A Memoir*, translated by Maureen Freely (London: Verso, 2008), p. 102.

17 Totovents, *Scenes from an Armenian Childhood*, p. 62.

18 Vahan Totovents, *Tell Me, Bella: A Selection of Stories*, translated by Mischa Kudian (London: Mashtots Press, 1972), p. 127.

19 G. W. Abgarian, *The Matenadaran* (Yerevan: Armenian State Publishing House, 1962), p. 6.

20 Christina Maranci, 'The Art and Architecture of Baghesh/Bitlis and Taron/Mush' in *Armenian Baghesh/Bitlis and Taron/Mush*, edited by Richard G. Hovannisian (Costa Mesa, California: Mazda Publishers, Inc., 2001), pp.119-46 (p. 125).

21 *Arménie: La magie de l'écrit*, edited by Claude Mutafian (Paris: Somogy editions d'art, 2007), p. 84.

22 *Jesus, Son, Only-Begotten of the Father: A Prayer by Nerses the Grace-filled, Armenian Catholicos 1100-1173*, translated by Jane S. Wingate (New York: The Delphic Press, 1947), [p. 9].

23 Donald Bloxham, *The Great Game of Genocide: Imperialism, Nationalism, and the Destruction of the Ottoman Armenians* (Oxford: Oxford University Press, 2005), p. 20.

24 Quoted in Edward Alexander, *A Crime of Vengeance: An Armenian*

Epilogue

It was the last evening of my fourth and possibly my final visit to Armenia. My companions had gone to see the famous dancing fountains in Yerevan's Republic Square and enjoy a last glass or two of Armenian brandy. I remained in my hotel room, keeping vigil in the twilight. Through the window Mount Ararat gradually vanished into the darkness. The twentieth-century Armenian poet Avetik Issahakian wrote:

> On the ancient peak of Ararat
> The centuries have come like seconds,
> And passed on.
>
> The eyes of generations dreading death
> Have glanced at its luminous summit,
> And passed on.
>
> The turn is now yours for a brief while:
> You, too, look at its lofty brow,
> And pass on![1]

I thought of Ceiriog writing about our Welsh mountains:

> The great mountains remain,
> the wind roars over them ...
>
> but there are new shepherds
> on these old mountains.[2]

I might easily have sunk into gloomy sentimentality, but then I remembered the monumental sculpture in

Stepanakert that the Armenians of Nagorno-Karabagh have made the symbol of their identity: 'We are our Mountains'. Resilience, courage, creativity, faith and a determination to pass on a uniquely valuable God-given heritage are what link Armenia and Wales: two mountainous lands at either end of Christendom. The Armenians have suffered more than almost any other people on earth – and yet they have survived. We have much to learn from them. Discovering Armenian history, spirituality and culture has been one of the most profoundly enriching experiences of my life. I commend it to my fellow *Cymry*.

Postscript

When I wrote this Epilogue I assumed that I would not be returning to Armenia. However, in November 2011 I went back there with a group of delightful Armenian pilgrims from England, Wales and Ireland, attending the episcopal consecration and ordination of Bishop Vahan Hovhanessian at Holy Etchmiadzin. I suspect now that it was not my final visit there. The spiritual light beyond Ararat has a powerful and lasting attraction.

Notes

[1]   Avetik Issahakian, *Selected Works: Poetry and Prose*, translated by Mischa Kudian (Moscow: Progress Publishers, no date), p. 21.

[2]   John Ceiriog Hughes, *Oriau'r Bore: Llyfr II* (Wrexham: Hughes & Son, no date), p. 50.

Further reading

Taner Akçam, *A Shameful Act: The Armenian Genocide and the Question of Turkish Responsibility* (New York: Metropolitan Books, 2006)

Grigoris Balakian, *Armenian Golgotha: A Memoir of the Armenian Genocide, 1915-1918* (New York: Alfred A. Knopf, 2009)

Peter Balakian, *The Burning Tigris: The Armenian Genocide* (London: William Heinemann, 2004)

Agop Hacikyan (co-ordinating editor), *The Heritage of Armenian Literature*, 3 vols (Detroit: Wayne State University Press, 2000-2002)

Tatul Hakobyan, *Karabagh Diary: Green and Black – Neither War nor Peace* (Antelias, Lebanon: The Author, 2010)

Robert H. Hewsen, *Armenia: An Historical Atlas* (Chicago: University of Chicago Press, 2001)

Nicholas Holding with Deirdre Holding, *Armenia with Nagorno Karabagh*, third edition (Chalfont St Peter, Bradt Travel Guides, 2011)

Vrej Nersessian, *Treasures from the Ark: 1700 Years of Armenian Christian Art* (London: The British Library, 2001)

Razmik Panossian, *The Armenians: From Kings and Priests to Merchants and Commissars* (London: Hurst & Co, 2006)

Iris Papazian (editor), *Karekin I: The Gift of Faith* (London: Karekin I Theological and Armenological Studies Series, 2009)

Simon Payaslian, *The History of Armenia* (New York: Palgrave Macmillan, 2007)

Huberta von Voss (editor), *Portraits of Hope: Armenians in the Contemporary World* (New York, Berghahn Books, 2007)